940. 54124.

30
24
29
10 ʃA.

Fighting Hitler from Dunkirk to D-Day

To all those millions of boys and girls, who left their homes during 1939–45 to answer the call to defend freedom. To those who should have been rewarded for bravery, but were not. I am sure they all did their best. You cannot ask for more than that.

Fighting Hitler from Dunkirk to D-Day

The Story of Die Hard Jeff Haward

Jeff Haward MM and Neil Barber

Pen & Sword
MILITARY

First published in Great Britain in 2015 by
Pen & Sword Military
an imprint of
Pen & Sword Books Ltd
47 Church Street
Barnsley
South Yorkshire
S70 2AS

Copyright © Neil Barber and Jeff Haward 2015

ISBN 978 1 47382 699 1

Typeset in Ehrhardt by
Mac Style Ltd, Bridlington, East Yorkshire
Printed and bound in the UK by CPI Group (UK) Ltd,
Croydon, CRO 4YY

Pen & Sword Books Ltd incorporates the imprints of Pen & Sword
Archaeology, Atlas, Aviation, Battleground, Discovery, Family
History, History, Maritime, Military, Naval, Politics, Railways,
Select, Transport, True Crime, and Fiction, Frontline Books, Leo
Cooper, Praetorian Press, Seaforth Publishing and Wharncliffe.

For a complete list of Pen & Sword titles please contact
PEN & SWORD BOOKS LIMITED
47 Church Street, Barnsley, South Yorkshire, S70 2AS, England
E-mail: enquiries@pen-and-sword.co.uk
Website: www.pen-and-sword.co.uk

Contents

Preface

The expression 'Die-Hard' is normally used to denote an individual or group of people who will not budge from a position or opinion once taken or expressed. Maybe the stand taken is not logically sound, but the fact remains that if the person refuses to retreat and holds out against all odds he is called a 'Die-Hard'. This term was first coined on 16 May 1811 during the bloodiest battle of the Peninsula War [1807–1812], at the Spanish town of Albuhera. Britain, Spain and Portugal were allied against the French forces of Napoleon Bonaparte. At Albuhera the Allies, under Marshal Beresford, faced the French Army commanded by Marshal Soult.

During this battle the 57th Regiment of Foot was outnumbered by four to one. The Commanding Officer, Colonel William Inglis took up position in front of his 'Fighting Villains' as he called them. During the subsequent fighting he was hit in the neck and left breast by grape shot from the French artillery, but adamantly refused to be carried to the rear for treatment. He remained with the Colours, exalting his men to *'Die hard the 57th, die hard!'* and die hard they did. Of the 570 other ranks, the Regiment suffered 420 casualties, while twenty of the thirty officers became casualties. Marshal Beresford wrote afterwards, *'Our dead, particularly the 57th Regiment, were lying as they fought in the ranks, every wound in front.'* Even after this savage fight and such appalling casualties, the survivors were apparently eager to advance with the remainder of the Army, but Beresford called out, *'Stop, stop the 57th, it would be a sin to let them go on!'*

After word of Colonel Inglis' actions became known, the soldiers of Wellington's Army dubbed the 57th Regiment 'The Die-Hards' and henceforth, they were always known as such.

The 57th Regiment of Foot was later renamed The Middlesex Regiment. It was the only regiment in the world whose nickname became part of the native language.

Chapter One

Upbringing

On 16 November 1937, at the age of eighteen, I walked down to the local Army Drill Hall in Hornsey, North London. After passing the medical and filling out various forms, a former Guards Regimental Sergeant Major called Coulsden, held out a shilling. I took it and from that moment there was no way back. I had joined a Territorial Machine-Gun battalion, the 1/7th Middlesex. I was now a 'Die Hard'!

* * *

We were a small family and during my growing up I never knew exactly why, not that I thought about it too much. Jeanne Catherine Elise Favez, my mother, was born in Lausanne, the French-speaking part of Switzerland. Her family wanted her to learn English, but without wealth the only way it could be done was to go 'into service'. Therefore, at around the turn of the twentieth century while in her late teens, she came across to England and found such employment in a large house in Finchley, North London.

My father, Arthur Haward, worked for R. Whites Mineral Waters, delivering lemonade around the area on a horse and cart and it was through these calls that they actually met. When they eventually decided to get married, my mother's parents told her that if she married this Englishman, they would have nothing further to do with her. My father's parents said exactly the same thing! They were married in 1911, but both families kept to their word and neither ever had the slightest thing to do with us.

I was born at 24 Beaconsfield Cottages, Long Lane, Finchley on 28 July 1919. This address was one in a row of small houses owned by my mother's employer in-service and when she got married, let it to my parents.

I had a brother and two sisters. Arthur was the eldest, being about eight years older, Marie was next in line and then Joan who was four years older than me.

My father had fought in The Great War, initially in the Royal Fusiliers, but then transferring to the Buffs. He lost a leg at Passchendaele and was invalided out. After recovering from his amputation, he was given a false leg and went back to work for R. Whites. This was fine while they used the horse and cart, particularly as the horse knew where to stop and start! Unfortunately, he had to give it up when the Company became mechanized and employed lorries.

There was an incident that occurred one summer when he was sitting in an old rocking chair. A fly had settled on his head and I decided to knock it off with a hammer! I don't recall the repercussions, but they must have been a bit violent because that is my only real memory of him. In 1927, he died from Hodgkin's disease, aged forty-six.

For a few years after this, things must have been tough for my mother, when life was hard anyway, because the owner of the house would come around for the weekly rent, and I often recall him saying, '*Put that back in your pocket. Don't tell anyone.*'

The money situation would not have improved when just after leaving school, Arthur was caught scrumping and went before the magistrate who informed him that he could either go to prison or join the Army. He joined the Army and went into the 1st Light Anti-Aircraft Regiment, Royal Artillery. They were subsequently sent to India and stationed at Peshawar on the Khyber Pass, a strange posting considering the distinct lack of aircraft in the vicinity.[1]

_____

1. He served in India for about seven years before coming home, only to be called up after a year on the Reserve when the war broke out. He was then sent out to North Africa and took part in the fighting around Gazala. When he came back, he was made up to a PSI, Permanent Staff Instructor on anti-aircraft matters.

However, some time after, my mother became involved with a door-to-door salesman whose wife had passed away. He sold tea towels, items of clothing and suchlike. Arthur was obviously away but Marie and Joan were dead against this chap. Anyway, eventually a younger brother, Norman, arrived!

Before I began school Scarlet Fever was prevalent and very contagious. My sister caught it and had to go into an isolation hospital at a place called Coney Hatch. When she came out, of course I caught it and suffered red blotches, so it was my turn for a spell in an isolation hospital, this being at Coppetts Wood, in the area of Friern Barnet. I spent about three weeks in there and during the morning on which I was to be discharged, my left ear clicked and felt peculiar. I noticed a discharge on the pillow, but really wanted to go home so I just turned it over. The two nurses who came to change the bed never saw it. I went home, but still had to be in quarantine for another three weeks after being discharged. A few days later the area behind my ear began to swell, very quickly leaving me with a lump the size of a chicken's egg that pushed my ear down and back. My mother decided to go and see a doctor who went around visiting schools. Squire's Lane School was close by, on a lane that led up to the old Squire's House itself. She described the symptoms and he told her that it could be very serious. Mum had Norman in a pushchair and had to walk back home, but the doctor did not want to wait, so he asked for the key to our house and immediately drove there. When I heard the lock go I thought it was my mother, but he called out for me and I hid behind the settee. Eventually of course, I was found and told that he was taking me to hospital in his car. On the way, as soon as he could, the doctor stopped and telephoned ahead because I still needed to be in quarantine, so I ended up back in the isolation hospital. My problem was very serious. I was suffering from mastoiditis, an infection that affected the air cells behind the ear. If not treated very quickly, it would be fatal. A special surgeon had to be brought in and he operated on me that night. I was put out with ether. A type of cage was laid over my face and a sponge squeezed against it from which dripped the ether. The surgeon said, '*Can you count to ten? I want you to count from ten backwards.*' I started counting and got less than halfway when everything started to get hot and go red. And then it exploded in my head and I felt myself sinking down.

The operation was successful but left me with a big scar behind the ear. The doctor told me that if I had left it much longer, it would have indeed been fatal.

When I reached five years of age, I attended Squire's Lane School.[2] The Headmaster was a Mr North, a strict disciplinarian, but very fair. He taught me a lot and I particularly enjoyed Geography. Another very strict teacher, Mr Hackett, had been in the Machine-Gun Corps during The Great War. The teachers had to be called Mister and Miss, and you were not allowed to do *anything* wrong. If you did, the result was a whack with a ruler or something similar. Things like not paying attention, in any way, brought a slap across the hand with a cane. In the woodwork class the teacher, who always said to us, '*Remember, you've only got one set of hands. Be careful. If you damage a hand, you'll never get another one,*' would not tolerate slacking or doing anything you should not have been. If anyone did, he would pick up a small piece of wood and throw it at the culprit! They were good teachers though.

I had a small group of friends. My best friend, John Suddes, also lived in the lane, while two others were around the corner. Another mate, Charlie Howard, was further up Long Lane. We would all meet, then go to Charlie's, and taking his family dog, walk across country all the way to Whetstone and go right the way around in a circle. There was also a bit of ground at the bottom of Squire's Lane called *The Rough Lots*, and we had a bit of a time chasing the girls around there, or really them chasing us! Nothing serious. There was little to do really, you had to make your own entertainment.

---

2. Before I left, the school changed its name to Manor House School.

I had a paper round at a well-known shop called Straker's. This was done before I went to school and on foot, as I did not have a bike. You just had to be strong enough to carry the bag containing all the papers. It did not pay much but I still gave Mum half of it.

People from local businesses used to visit the school to interview the leavers, but as I neared school leaving age there was not a lot of work about, so I was lucky to be offered something. And so, at fourteen years of age I left school on the Friday and started work the following Monday in a factory in East Finchley. The company was called Sims Bakelite and they made all sorts of items, as Bakelite was all the rage. My job was working on cigarette holders. After manufacture there was a seam where the two moulds met and I had to remove the seam so that it was smooth. The place had such a horrible, oppressive smell that I left after a fortnight and got another job in an electrical factory in Whetstone called Sildon Radio. In all electrical plugs there are three screws and it was my task was to fit the screws by turning them two or three threads so that they would not fall out! It was so monotonous that I did not stay there for long either. Just up the road from home was a family plumbing firm called Kilners, so I applied there and was told that I would be taken on if I entered a seven-year apprenticeship, with the last of those years being spent as what they called an 'Improver', working under supervision. I also had to go to Willesden Technical College for one night a week to learn the theory side. However, when things in the country got bad and there was not a lot of work coming in, I left and got another job with Charlie Howard at a firm building Council flats all over London. I spent most of my time in the East End, mainly the Hackney area. The houses were very basic. None had plaster on the walls, just the rendering.

There was a bloke who lived up the road who I had met at Sildon Radio called Sid Young. He persuaded me to join the Territorials.[3] I thought it would be something to do in the evenings and of course

---

3. Ironically, when it came to mobilisation, Sid was not classed as A1 in the fitness test, and so was posted to do an administrative job!

to go away on a fortnight's camp once a year was very attractive. The Hornsey Drill Hall in Priory Road was actually the home of 'C' Company and Company Headquarters of the 1/7th Middlesex. The other Companies that comprised the battalion were located in Highgate, Wood Green and Edmonton.

The first night that I went home after receiving my uniform, I could see from the look on my mother's face that she was uncomfortable with it, and said that it was something she did not really want to see. Obviously what had happened to my father had affected her deeply.

Training took place every Friday evening. There was no pay, only travelling expenses from Finchley to the Drill Hall.

* * *

As with all battalions, the 1/7th Middlesex was commanded by a Lieutenant Colonel, who had a Major as his second-in-command. The battalion had five Companies, 'A', 'B', 'C', 'D' and HQ, each commanded at that time by a Captain (although this was to change to a Major as we reached our war establishment). The Company was equipped with the Vickers Medium machine gun and with the four Companies each having twelve such machine guns, the battalion possessed some formidable firepower.

Each Company was broken down into three platoons, 'C' Company's being numbered 10, 11 and 12. I was in 12 Platoon. The Platoon Commander was a 2nd Lieutenant and there was also a Platoon Sergeant, a range-taker, a runner to take messages, a First-Aid man and a cook. The 12 Platoon Commander was Lieutenant Victor Scantlebury.[4]

Platoon transport consisted of six Morris Commercial 15cwt trucks, one each for the machine guns, one for the Platoon Commander and

---

4. Lieutenant Scantlebury was later transferred to the 1st Middlesex Battalion and was killed in action out in the Far East on Christmas Day 1941, aged 24. He is commemorated on the Sai Wan Memorial in Hong Kong.

one for the Platoon Sergeant who had all the stores. This truck did not have a Vickers, but carried one Bren gun for anti-aircraft fire. The cook also travelled on this vehicle which always brought up the rear. These trucks had dedicated drivers.

Such a platoon consisted of two Sections, each having two Vickers guns. A Section had a Section Commander, this being a Corporal. In theory, a Gun Crew comprised five men; the Number 1, being a Corporal, fired the Vickers while the Number 2 fed the ammunition to the gun, and the Numbers 3, 4 and 5 maintained a constant supply of ammunition. However, due to the shortage of men a Gun Crew was fortunate to have three, let alone five men. Instead, we used the drivers.

Training on the machine guns was minimal because in reality our instructors knew nothing about the Vickers and the only way we could be taught how to use them was from the training manuals. Therefore, most of our time was spent discussing the availability of the local girls and drinking cheap beer in the canteen.

The first year's camp was situated at Arundel in Sussex. Our time was spent wandering up and down hills following tapes that were put out for night attacks. A Colonel called Pringle who had won the Military Cross in the Great War was riding around on a horse, while even at that stage the Germans were driving about in tanks.

Although war was looming we never seriously discussed it or thought about the implications. The signs were there when Hitler took the Sudetenland and then Czechoslovakia, and Mussolini had invaded Abyssinia and Albania, but we believed 'it couldn't happen to us'.

* * *

On Friday 1 September 1939 Germany invaded Poland. I was working in a house at Finsbury Park near the Arsenal football ground when the news came out. We were fixing a big water tank and I said to the foreman, '*I don't think I'll be in tomorrow Joe.*' He said, '*No, I don't suppose you will!*' Sure enough, that same day the BBC announced general mobilisation and the order for all Reservists and Territorial Army Units to report to their respective barracks or depot. I went home and packed, but there was not any real goodbye scene between my mother and I. It was all a bit embarrassing so I thought 'the sooner I get away the better'.

On the following Sunday, war was actually declared. Nobody knew quite what to think. For the previous few months, cinemas had been showing a weekly series in the *Pathe News* that explained the different armies and their armaments, and how smug the French were, sitting in their Maginot Line. Nothing could ever get past them. It also showed what people thought a Second World War would be like. The impression given by the film series was that the country was going to be wiped out almost immediately by mass air raids, so we all expected the worst.

The next three weeks were spent in the Drill Hall, sleeping on the hard floor with a solitary blanket. Trenches were dug outside on the tennis courts, we had our vaccinations, did indoor training on the machine guns, and carried out driving practice on the 15cwt trucks, all around the Alexandra Palace. Whenever we marched through the streets behind our band we were showered with kisses and free beer. I thought 'this war can't be too bad'. Mobilisation also meant that we actually got paid. As a Private I was given fourteen shillings a week and again, gave my mother half of that, but it was quite a drop in wages because previously I had been earning £5 a week.

On 14 October the Middlesex Companies marched from their respective Drill Halls to Wood Green Station where two special trains took us to the grim reality of the Victorian 'Salamanca Barracks' at Aldershot. The whole battalion of 27 officers and 609 other ranks concentrated here and shortly after, the arrival of 131 militiamen from the Machine-Gun Training Company, Mill Hill, brought the unit up to virtually full strength.[5]

---

5. Although I did not know it at the time, on 1 November at 5pm, the battalion was put on eight hours notice to move to East Anglia in the event of an invasion. Verbal orders were given to the Company Commanders otherwise the matter was to be kept secret. All leave was stopped.

Normal training plus weapons training began almost immediately and everyone suffered at the hands of a corporal, a Middlesex Reservist. He was one of the most objectionable, foul-mouthed people I had ever met. He went out of his way to make everyone's life a misery. When referring to the war, he continually barracked us with his two favourite sayings; '*This will sort the men from the boys*' and '*When we get there, it will be the survival of the fittest.*'

While here, we received sixteen vehicles that were meant to represent the 30cwt trucks stipulated on the war establishment, but were actually civilian vehicles impressed into use, ranging in size up to 5 Tons. Further 15cwt trucks were issued later in the month.[6]

Here I met a chap called Frank Dollin. He was slightly older than me, married, with a little girl. Frank was the Number 1 on the gun and we just clicked and became firm friends.

After four months of training by Regular Army instructors we just about knew our left foot from our right and which end of a gun the bullets came out.

---

6. 1 cwt is 112lbs. 2240lbs is 1 Ton.

Chapter Two

With the British Expeditionary Force
in France

O n 13 January 1940 we were shipped from Southampton to France on what was a cross-channel ferry, landing at Cherbourg. The battalion immediately boarded a train which had proper carriages, not the *'40 Hommes, 20 Chevaux'* type from the First World War! Snow was falling and it was very cold.

During the journey, on one occasion when we were informed that the train was stopping for half an hour, a lot of the blokes got off and went into a café, an *estaminet*. They all began drinking some type of 'rot gut'. I decided not to touch it. Eventually our sergeant, who had rather a drop too much, was hanging over the back of the seat, singing. I just thought 'For Christ's sake shut up and go to sleep!'

We continued on the train for a couple more days and the journey ended at a place near Le Mans, where there was a three-day stay. While there we *all* went out for a drink at an *estaminet*. None of us was used to French alcohol. This particular café was set up high and had steps down either side but nothing at the front. The owner could see what was going to happen and was quite amused when we all fell through the front and landed in the road. A truck had to come and pick everyone up to get us back to the billet. The next day we boarded open backed 15cwt Bedford trucks and headed towards the French – Belgian border. Everyone was ill. I had never felt so terrible in all my life and swore never to touch another drop of cognac. The weather was absolutely freezing and in the truly arctic conditions, it took three days to travel the 300 miles to reach our destination of Gondecourt, near Lille.

* * *

The British Expeditionary Force had been moved to this area for a specific reason. During the 1930s Belgium had performed a delicate diplomatic balancing act in order to ensure its status as a neutral country, and had therefore not had any level of military consultation with the British or French. However, as the German threat became more apparent, Belgium developed a defensive system and a plan in the event of such an invasion. With its eastern frontier being around 200 kilometres long, it was impossible to defend the whole length against what would be far stronger German forces. Consequently, the initial phase was to be a delaying action. In the north, the barrier of the Albert Canal, protected at its eastern end by the fortress of Eben Emael, would provide the initial delaying position. At a certain stage, these forces would then fall back, destroying bridges, roads and railways as they went, to a prepared defensive line between the fortified towns of Antwerp and Namur. This line began just east of Antwerp at Koningshoyckt, and went south, passing through Malines and Louvain, ending in the town of Wavre. This was known as the KW Line (Koningshoyckt – Wavre) and possessed a continuous anti-tank barrier with many strongpoints. Preparations had also been made to flood certain areas. The plan meant leaving almost half of the country in German hands but there was simply no other option.

In January 1940, a Messerchmitt 108 aircraft carrying a Major Hellmuth Reinberger landed in fog at Mechelin in Belgium. He was carrying secret documents relating to the German invasion of Holland and Belgium. These were duly passed to the Dutch and French authorities. Subsequently, General Maurice Gamelin, Commander-in-Chief of the French Army, devised a plan that would try to help the Dutch and also dovetail the French and British forces into the Belgian Plan.

An agreement was reached with Belgium that once attacked, the British and French would move into the country to occupy positions on the River Dyle defence line, south of Antwerp. The Belgian Army would defend the area from Antwerp to the north of Louvain, the BEF

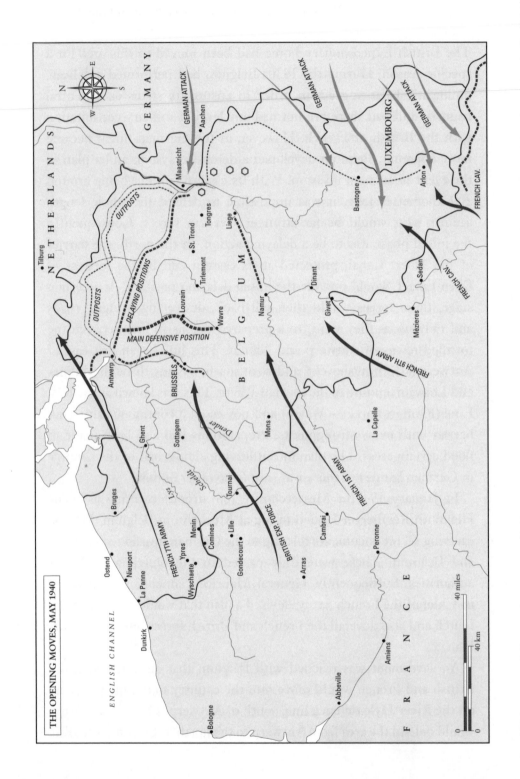

THE OPENING MOVES, MAY 1940

ENGLISH CHANNEL

NETHERLANDS

GERMANY

GERMAN ATTACK

Aachen

Maastricht

Tilburg

OUTPOSTS

OUTPOSTS

DELAYING POSITIONS

St. Trond

Tongres

Tirlemont

Louvain

Wavre

MAIN DEFENSIVE POSITION

Antwerp

BRUSSELS

B E L G I U M

Ghent

Sottegem

Dender

Mons

La Capelle

Bruges

Schèldt

Menin

Tournai

Comines

Lille

Ypres

Wyschaete

Gondecourt

Cambrai

Arras

Peronne

FRENCH 1ST ARMY

BRITISH EXP. FORCE

FRENCH 7TH ARMY

L35

Ostend

Nieuport

La Panne

Dunkirk

Bologne

Abbeville

Amiens

F R A N C E

Liège

Namur

Dinant

Givet

Mézieres

Sedan

FRENCH 9TH ARMY

LUXEMBOURG

GERMAN ATTACK

GERMAN ATTACK

Bastogne

Arlon

FRENCH CAV.

FRENCH CAV.

N
E
W
S

0   40 miles

0   40 km

would hold the line between Louvain and Wavre, while the French First Army moved into position from Wavre to the border town of Givet. South of this point the French would advance towards Neufchateau. In aid of the Dutch, the French Seventh Army was to advance from the direction of Dunkirk to occupy the south-western section of Holland, around Breda. These positions were expected to be occupied by the third day of the war.

With the Maginot Line securing the French frontier, this was to be the area where the invasion was halted.

*   *   *

Our time at Gondecourt was spent in farms, the sleeping arrangements being located in the roofs of barns. It remained freezing cold. There was ice on the rafters and all we had was the straw and a blanket. It was so cold that one morning I went to clean my teeth and the toothpaste had frozen solid. We stayed there for what was a long winter drinking French beer and eating egg and chips.

I still didn't know much about Army food. When the cook started to give out biscuits that I had never encountered before, I took one and was asked if I wanted another. Thinking it was a kind of digestive I took another one, went to bite it and nearly broke a tooth. These biscuits were about three inches square and so hard that they had to be broken with a hammer and then sucked! The cook was an old soldier who, due to his hair, we called 'Sandy', mainly because it irritated him no end. For dinner he gave us stew every day for six months. One day someone said to him, '*It tastes a bit better today. Did you find a dirty stick to stir it with?*' His only answer was '*You don't like it? Leave it.*'

*   *   *

During February, the CO, Colonel Pringle, was shifted to an administrative job and we received a new Commanding Officer, Lieutenant Colonel B. B. Rackham. It was he who made our battalion, turning us from a load of 'Saturday Night Soldiers' as we were known, into quite an efficient fighting unit. We also had a good Company Commander, Captain John Panks.

The Vickers machine guns had the task of firing over the heads of our advancing infantry. However, although we knew the basics, I would not have liked to advanced beneath us! In fact, the 1/7th Middlesex had been so badly trained that we were attached to the 2nd Battalion, The Middlesex Regiment, a Regular Army battalion, in order to intensify our training. This battalion was part of the 3rd Infantry Division, of which Major General Bernard Montgomery was the Divisional Commander. Their NCOs began to arrive daily and train us, and it was they who actually taught us how to fire the gun.

*   *   *

The Vickers Medium Machine Gun was quite a weapon. It basically comprised the gun, a tripod and a water condensing can. The weapon was broken down for transportation and reassembled for action. The setting up operation was very complicated. The gun was fitted on the tripod, which then had to be tightened with a clamp. Each gun was slightly different and so you had to know exactly how much to tighten the clamp. Consequently, each crew kept the gun it was issued with, unless of course it was damaged by enemy action, when a replacement was supplied.

To load it, a canvas fibre ammunition belt was fed through the feed block and pulled slightly to the front.[1] There was a crank handle on the side of the gun that had to be pulled back twice. The first time took the bullet from the belt onto the face of what was called the lock.

There were two pawls on the front of the lock that actually grabbed the back of the cartridge and pulled the round from the belt and

---

1. Before the war began, we had received ammunition that was held together by metal links, but these were quickly replaced by cloth fibre webbing belts. Once fired, they were discarded but had to be re-used, so these would be collected later by Line of Communication troops.

dropped it in line with the barrel. The crank handle was allowed to return to the forward position, and the second time it was pulled, it pushed the bullet up the barrel. At the same time another round was pulled out of the belt and into the lock. Then it was ready to fire.

The Vickers was actually fired with the thumbs. It had two grips with wooden handles and you put your fingers around them while two other fingers held up the safety catch, which was quite large. Both thumbs pressed a firing button that protruded from the end of the gun. When pressed, the firing pin moved forward with the lock and struck the percussion cap of the cartridge, initiating the propellant within and sending the bullet up the barrel. The Number 2 had to steady the canvas belt because it vibrated up and down and the bullets had to go through evenly. Unless the belt went in straight, the pawls would not get hold of the bullet and the gun jammed. If this did occur, to clear the jam the Number 1 pulled the belt to the left rear and gave the crank handle a tap which would generally do the job. This had to be done twice, once to clear the jammed round and again to place another in position.

When firing, the barrel quickly became hot and so was enclosed by a water-filled cylindrical metal jacket to cool it. When this water condensed to steam, it passed through a valve on the front of the gun, down a piece of tube, into a condenser can, which in fact was an old two-gallon petrol can. The steam then returned to water. When necessary, this water could be used to refill the water jacket via a filler cap on the top of the gun.

It could also leak where the barrel fed through the water jacket. The only way to keep the water jacket relatively watertight was to apply asbestos string around the barrel. The exterior of the barrel was tapered, being wider at the muzzle end. About two inches from the end, a groove of between a quarter and half an inch depth was cut into the taper. The asbestos string was rolled between the hands with a small amount of rifle oil until it was soft and from the groove, wound around the jacket as tightly as possible while being tapped with a wooden handle of a screwdriver, so that it fitted inside the jacket. Once fitted, a little water would still be lost, so it had to be topped up.

There were twenty-eight possible stoppages on a Vickers. About five of them were very common, such as a broken firing pin or fuzee spring, but all of the possibilities had to be learnt. The firing pin had a little round piece on the end that was constantly striking the percussion cap in the rear of the cartridge. Ultimately, the pin either broke off or became flattened and would not make the right contact on the cap.

The fuzee spring, a tiny item, worked the crank handle that went up and down. The spring could break or become so weak that the crank handle could not do its job properly.

The Number 2 carried a parts bag with a few tools and spare pieces such as the lock. The spare would be fitted and the broken one given to the Number 3 who either repaired it or had it replaced. This was the procedure for all components such as the firing pin and spring.

The barrel had to be changed every 10,000 rounds due to the rifling becoming worn and this took between two and three minutes.

We all believed that it was the best gun, because provided it was oiled and the water jacket around the barrel kept full of water, it would go on forever. If it was dropped in the mud it would still go, unlike the Bren which refused to work if it got a little bit of dirt in it.

It used .303-inch ammunition, common to many British weapons, but fired the bullets in a different manner to any other machine gun. Whereas a burst of fire from a light machine gun such as a Bren formed a small circle, a Vickers fired into a 'beaten zone', a pear shape, and the greater the range the bigger the zone.[2]

A normal burst from a Vickers, which was five seconds, twenty-five rounds, would be spread out over a large area. This type of fire usually

---

2. The Bren's curved 30-round magazine was never fully loaded. This was because there was a spring at the top of the magazine and sometimes it would jam at critical moments. You did not get a second chance, so there was no room for mistakes. Therefore only twenty-eight rounds were loaded.

employed a number of guns and was called a 'pepperpot shoot'. In fact the Vickers was nicknamed 'the pepperpot'. And so, ideally, to make the most effective use of the Vickers guns, their firepower needed to be coordinated. In order to get each of the four Section guns firing at the same target area, an aiming post would be placed in the ground about ten yards in front [depending on the ground, as it had to be able to be seen by each of the guns. If there were bushes, it might have to be placed closer.] This post protruded from the ground by about twelve inches and had a round disc on it of about three inches in diameter. The centre was white and the outside ring black.

To set up each gun against the firing post, there was the Dial Foresight, which was similar to that used by the artillery. For this, a Director, the Platoon Commander, would give the orders. The device had various dials and so to ensure that every dial was at zero before anything was started, the first order was '*Zero dials*'. Next was '*All on the aiming post*' which meant aiming the prismic sight of the dial at the aiming post. The Platoon range taker calculated from a map, the distance to the target. Then it was '*Range*' and so many yards, followed by the angle of sight. Then '*Elevation*'. The Platoon Commander worked out the elevation to take the bullets where they were intended to go. On elevation, the further the distance to the target, the lower the trajectory. If the target was closer then the barrel had to be elevated as obviously the rounds had the same sized charge and this had to be used up.

There also had to be an allowance for wind, because it would take the bullets in flight. Then it would be '*Number 1 gun, left five degrees. Number 2 gun, left two degrees*,' while the two guns on the right would be told to aim accordingly in that direction. This was all to cover an area.[3]

---

3. At the beginning of the war we had what was known as the Bar Foresight. There were two sights that had to be opened on the Vickers, a big one at the back and a small one at the front. The Bar Foresight was clipped on the one at the back. The Vickers could be raised or lowered as required by turning a wheel of a threaded shaft on the tripod. This Bar Foresight was attached to the right hand side of the gun and the level of the barrel checked by the spirit level within the sight itself.

This fine adjustment to the direction of the gun was done by tapping. Holding the gun with one hand, the handle was glanced with the palm of the other. Experience taught the gunner exactly how heavy a tap was required to shift it by one degree, left or right.

To cover an area, a normal five-second burst would be fired. If the gun was on the left of the Section the handle was given 'left, one tap,' then another burst, another tap, another burst. Then the gun was to return to its original position using the same number of taps so that the same area was covered. The next gun covered the area beside it and so on.

There could also be 'Method of Fire' such as rapid fire where a belt was fired straight off, or so many belts per gun if it was 'Harassing' fire. It was also possible to receive the order, 'Gun control' which was only employed if the fighting got a bit close! Then, the Corporal firing the gun would pick his own target, sort out the situation and then go back to being under control.

To provide such fire support, we were generally in the second line, following the advancing infantry, usually by truck, but for the occasions when they were unable to reach us, we had to do what was called a 'long carry', moving them by hand. The Number 1 carried the tripod, placing the two front legs over the shoulders and the rear leg down the back. The Number 2 carried the Vickers gun across his shoulders, plus the spare parts bag. The tripod weighed about 56lbs and the gun weight was the same with a gallon of water, which is 10lbs on its own, so they were pretty heavy. Numbers 3, 4 and 5 all carried a thousand rounds of ammunition, four metal boxes, each containing a 250-round belt.

Such was the use and intricacies of the Vickers.

* * *

Our routine at Gondecourt ended on Friday 10 May 1940, when the Platoon Sergeant, Lenney, told us to pack up and get on the 15cwt trucks. We were moving into Belgium. During the early hours of the morning the Germans had invaded the Netherlands, Luxembourg and

Belgium. We immediately headed for our pre-determined position of Louvain on the River Dyle and continued driving through the night. It was still dark when we crossed the border. Driving in the dark was a tricky operation and the only help for the drivers was a light fitted to the rear axle beneath the trucks. It was not exactly a bright light but visible enough for the following driver.

When daylight arrived, as we passed through the villages en-route, the occupants were waving and shouting at us, and seemed very pleased at our arrival.

We arrived at Louvain in the early hours of 11 May, where 'C' Company took up position in a suburb called Eichen. In our particular spot the majority of the civilians had already left, so it was decided to set up our gun in a house. There was an *estaminet* that was locked up, so Sergeant Lenney broke the lock and got in. Naturally, we began to sample the Belgian hospitality within. Unfortunately the owners, a married couple, returned and started screaming about our breaking in. They immediately went away and returned with a Belgian policeman. There was a bit of a set-to that culminated in us having to get out. The owner's wife was more worried about us paying for the drinks than about the advancing Germans.

Unbeknown to us the Eben Emael Fortress and various vital bridges in the area of the Albert Canal had been captured by the Germans. This had been achieved by employing a new form of warfare, the use of parachutists and gliderborne troops. The Belgians subsequently fought hard for thirty-six hours, even recapturing one of the bridges, however, the overwhelming forces, plus total mastery of the air by the *Luftwaffe*, threatened to surround these Belgian forces behind the canal when German tanks broke through near Tongres.

During the evening of 12 May the Belgians were ordered to withdraw to the Antwerp – Namur Line. These forces defending the canal and those who continued the struggle in the Fort of Liege, delayed the Germans long enough for the British and the French to take up position. Three British Divisions had advanced to hold the Louvain –

Wavre part of the line, with a further six Divisions set behind between the Dyle and Scheldt rivers.

The 1/7th Middlesex Battalion's first contact with the enemy came two days later when forward positions were shelled with shrapnel. The following day, there were probing attacks. 'C' Company did not get seriously engaged with the enemy, although some of our other units did. However, there was slight infiltration into Louvain by the enemy, but a counter-attack pushed them out. Having found our positions we experienced our first air raids by *Stuka* dive-bombers. Being an unknown, they were the most frightening thing to occur. There were always three or four of them that circled around before coming down, dropping their bombs and then heading off in all directions. However, we learned quickly. If the aircraft were fired at on their way down, they could see where this was coming from and one of the *Stukas* would peel off and drop a bomb on that spot. Consequently, we started to hold our fire for the first three, but then open up on the last one. He was already committed to his dive and could not re-adjust to drop a bomb in a different spot to that already chosen. In this way, one was eventually shot down.

During the evening of 17 May the order was given to retire to a position west of Brussels. As we moved back, there were already thousands of displaced people and the roads were crowded with them in every form of conveyance. There seemed to be a lot of scaremongering with every nun being a German. These refugees were mercilessly machine-gunned and bombed by the *Luftwaffe* to deliberately cause chaos on the roads, and delay us getting through them.

On this same day, after the terrible bombing of Rotterdam, the Dutch capitulated to avoid further civilian casualties.

During the afternoon of 18 May we pulled into a yard that was full with stacks of wood. Everyone was tired and I went into an office where there was an old horsehair sofa, so I laid down on it and fell asleep. The next thing I knew, there were bits of timber flying everywhere. The Germans had started shelling us and this was the first time I had come under such intense artillery fire. We got out of there a bit sharpish.

A familiar scenario began. We would retire, take up position anc ___... withdraw again. On each occasion, this was before getting seriously involved with stopping the enemy. No one seemed to understand why, but five days earlier the Germans had attacked the French positions south of Namur, between Houx and Sedan, with armoured spearheads breaking through at Sedan, about twenty miles beyond the western extent of the Maginot Line. During the evening of 15 May the French Ninth Army, the formation that was 'hinged' to the Maginot Line, had withdrawn from the Allied defensive line, forcing the decision to abandon the only organized position, and fall back to the Escault. The German pressure on the British and the Belgian Armies had just been intended to keep our forces pinned while their armour tore into the French and in effect, our rear. By rushing forward into Belgium, we had done exactly what the Germans had wanted us to do.

By 17 May, there was confusion in the French Command as to what was happening and exactly where the Germans were. In fact, they were beyond Vervins, fifty miles west of Sedan.

This pattern of retreat continued until we reached the River Dendre where the Company took up defensive positions on the west bank of the river itself. Our task was to cover the withdrawal of the infantry.

Sunday 19 May was the tenth day of the campaign and at first light Germans appeared on the east bank of the Dendre, but the bridge had already been destroyed, as I had heard the explosion after we fell back.

The next move was back towards the River Scheldt. The 1/7th was again part of the covering force, and 'C' Company was positioned in the area of the railway line running through Sottegem. We set up our Vickers on the platform of the station itself. This position was held until the following day when, after all of the infantry had passed through, we began our own withdrawal. On reaching the Scheldt, it was found that the Belgians were already behind it. Again, the Germans reached the opposite bank the following day, but this position was held for two days.

To the south, Tuesday 21 May saw the Germans capture Amiens on the Somme and then later in the day the railway junction at Abbeville.

However, a British Armoured attack took place towards Arras and although unsuccessful, it severely shook the Germans. Two days later, the overall situation was looking rather desperate with the German breakthrough in the south actually reaching the Channel port town of Boulogne, meaning that the northern part of the BEF was now in effect, cut off from its French Ally. During the morning the 1/7th Middlesex linked up with the 2nd Middlesex Battalion to man frontier defences at Wattrelos, Roubaix and Tourcoing.

Obviously, I knew none of this. We did an awful lot of moving about, but being a private, the powers that be never took me into their confidence. What I did know was that to our north, the Belgians continued to fall back without warning. Every time we dug-in to fight, the Belgians disappeared.

On 25 May the battalion now held a position at the French–Belgian border, between Bousbecque and Comines, opposite the town of Wervick on the River Lys. 12 Platoon was dug-in on the nearside bank, covering a road running along the far bank and the entrance to the village. With the Belgians having departed, the Colonel decided that he must know what was happening on the other side of the river, and so two dinghies were found and a scratch patrol of eight men assembled, led by Sergeant Burford. Covered by us, they rowed the thirty yards to the far bank and he positioned his men. After about ten minutes, to everyone's surprise a German soldier came cycling along the road. The sergeant shot him, pulling his body and the cycle into the ditch. Shortly after, a blue car came round the bend and Burford emptied his revolver into the car, killing the driver and front seat passenger. The rear door opened and an officer took a lightning leap out and ran off. Upon inspection of the car they found that this officer had left behind his cap, belt with Luger and briefcase. These were quickly gathered up as more German soldiers began to arrive and a brisk exchange of fire took place. One man was killed, one wounded and one ended up as missing [later found to have been captured], but covered by the fire of my platoon's four machine guns, Sergeant Burford was able to return to our side, bringing the wounded man with him.[4] The captured briefcase was immediately taken to the 3rd Division HQ.

Unfortunately, the following afternoon we were bombed and suffered a number of casualties, one of them being Sergeant Lenney. I picked up the barrel of his rifle. The butt and the rest of it had gone.[5]

That afternoon we were on the move again, this time to the north, to the Wyschaete Ridge, south of Ypres. The next day the ridge was heavily shelled and again there were casualties.

Meanwhile, the captured suitcase had been analysed at 3rd Division HQ and was found to belong to a certain Lieutenant Colonel Kinzel, an Intelligence Officer. Incredibly, it contained the order of battle and plans for the German Corps opposing us. These showed that the enemy's next intention was to attack the area of the join of the BEF and the Belgian Army between the towns of Ypres and Comines. This would enable them to advance around the left flank of the BEF. As Montgomery's staff had been poring over these documents, General Alan Brooke, the 2 Corps Commander had arrived. With the importance of the documents obviously apparent, he immediately made sure that they were passed to Lord Gort, Commander of the BEF.[6, 7]

This was such a windfall that there was indecision over the authenticity of the documents. Eventually, it was decided that the

---

4. Sergeant Burford was mentioned in despatches for this action.
5. Sergeant Cyril Lenney is buried at Wervicq [Sud] Communal Cemetery, Grave 1. He was aged 34.
6. According to Hugh Sebag-Montefiore in his book, 'Dunkirk: Fight to the Last Man', Kinzel was the Liaison Officer between the Commander in Chief of the Army, Field Marshal Walther von Brauchitsch and the Sixth Army's Commander, General Walther von Reichenau. I think that Kinzel may have survived the war because afterwards I read an account about matters in Berlin and it mentioned a General Kinzel. Whether or not it was the same man I don't know, but he certainly never got his shoe horn back!
7. The details of how this briefcase came to be analysed, Brooke's involvement and how the information was passed to Lord Gort [and the battle of the Ypres Comines Canal itself] is expertly described in Charles More's *The Road to Dunkirk*, Frontline Books, 2013.

plans were indeed genuine because the briefcase also contained a shoehorn, implying that Kinzel had tight jackboots. Consequently, on 27 May the 3rd Division made an amazing twenty-five mile sideways move that entailed cutting across the lines of communication of the 5th and 50th Divisions, a very difficult operation that only Montgomery could have carried out. Therefore, we were able to block the area that the Germans were going to attack through, and why we had moved to the Wyschaete Ridge.[8]

However, to the south, on the previous day the Germans had bypassed Calais and were positioned at Gravelines, only fourteen miles from the centre of Dunkirk. It was only on this day that the first preparations for Operation *Dynamo*, the evacuation of the BEF from France, began. The Line of Communications troops went first while the Line regiments were kept for defence of the perimeter.

Once again we were not in position for long as the battalion received orders to destroy all papers and kit and to withdraw to a strongpoint in the woods north of Poperinghe. Maps of the district were unobtainable and with all roads under very heavy attack by bombs and shellfire, the withdrawal became something of a nightmare. It was made even more difficult when a French Army Corps got mixed up with the British troops, but with considerable ingenuity and some excellent cross-country guesswork, the move was completed successfully.

In the early hours of 28 May the Belgians capitulated without warning, leaving our particular Division in a very precarious position with again, no defence on that flank. Therefore yet another rapid withdrawal was made, swinging round to take up positions on the Aa Canal near Nieuport on what was now the Dunkirk perimeter. In spite of all the withdrawals, for the first time I realized that something was seriously wrong when we were moving along a road and in a field

---

8. And so, if a 'Die Hard' sergeant had not managed to capture the plan, German Panzers could well have reached the beaches first and the outcome of Dunkirk may have been very different.

beside it were large French Howitzers. The French artillerymen had put wood around them and were setting them all alight.

After driving down this long straight road we arrived on the Aa during the afternoon. We pulled onto the side of the road and pooled the whole Company around the dozen 15cwt trucks. Everyone got out and was milling around, leaning against trees, when bursts of machine-gun fire came straight down the road from the direction we were travelling, ricocheting off the cobblestones. The Company had never moved so quickly. Most took cover in the ditches but I got behind a big tree. The firing went on for a while until someone shouted, '*We've got to turn the trucks around and go back.*' And so the drivers ran for their vehicles and began turning them round in the road. As soon as your particular driver was almost around, you got the word 'GO!' and everyone made a mad dash for the back of the trucks. It all became a bit hectic. I ran along the side of the road to where my truck was and jumped in the back with everyone else. I only know what happened to my truck. I didn't hang around to look out for the rest. You had to be quick or you got left behind. I think most managed to get out of it.

After dark we went back and took up position on the canal. Our instructions were to hold the canal while the evacuation was taking place and to cover a bridge that had been blown but could still be used, as the Germans had managed to send some fighting patrols across.

The battalion was fairly widely scattered, with Battalion Headquarters in Oost Dunkirk village, 'A' Company around Nieuport Bains, 'B' Company on the Wulpen road, 'C' Company around Nieuport Ville, and 'D' Company in the woods on the road to Oost Dunkirk Bains. Dunkirk itself was about eighteen miles away.

During darkness we went up to the bridge and I asked this sergeant, a Territorial, where to mount the gun. He said, '*Here, on the road,*' which was cobbled. We said, '*Well what are we going to aim at?*' '*That bridge down there.*' Frank Dollin said, '*What bridge? It's too dark to see any bridge.*' '*It's straight down there.*' Frank said, '*I'm not taking responsibility for firing at a bridge we can't see, especially with our own infantry around it.*' The sergeant got down on the gun and he tapped this way and that, and said, '*That's alright, it's on it now!*' We thought 'What are you bloody talking about? The sooner we get away from you the better!' Anyway, as soon as he disappeared into the night, we shifted the gun to the side of the road.

For the following few days we were under continuous heavy aerial and artillery attack, with enemy infantry patrols crossing the canal every night. There were a number of casualties, especially in 'C' Company, which suffered heavily. During this period, we saw a bloke sitting on the ground with no cover at all. Frank said to him, '*You had better get down.*' He didn't move and when Frank touched him, he was dead, just fell over.

Thankfully, the enemy did not make a determined attack, because we were not sure we could stop them if they did.

During the night of 31 May I was still on the Vickers with Frank Dollin. Enemy machine-gun tracer bullets were flying everywhere. Gradually, *Spandau* and machine-pistol fire started to come from behind.[9] A German patrol had broken through. Company Headquarters was a short distance behind us in a farmhouse and Frank said, '*We had better let them know that the Germans are behind us. Who'll volunteer to take a message back?*' I had a quick think and decided 'it was a lot better back there than sitting here', so I volunteered. I set off, running hell for leather up the side of the road. A burst of machine-gun fire came quite close, the bullets ricocheting off the cobbles. As I approached the farmhouse building, a bloke stepped out from around the corner. He just about shouted, '*Halt! Who goes there?*' before firing his rifle. We were only feet apart, and I could never have stopped. I was also so out of breath that I couldn't have said the password even if I had wanted to. There was a sting in my right arm and I was knocked onto my back. I

---

9. The range of the Vickers, over 4000 yards, was its only advantage over the German equivalent, the MG42, or Spandau as we knew it, so at times we could sit back a bit and have a game with them when they could not reach us. It used to annoy them!

then got up, telling him in a series of profanities exactly what I thought of him. It turned out to be a friend of mine, Johnny Hunt. Knowing that no German could swear like that, he then realized who I was and started apologizing. '*I aimed for your head, you know!*' I said '*Well it's a bloody good job you're a rotten shot!*' The bullet had glanced the top of my right arm and it was bleeding a bit. Each man carried a First-Aid dressing, a yellow pad with a bandage, which was kept in a special pocket. This was provided for personal use only and was not to be employed on anyone else. That was stressed to everyone. So that was wrapped around my arm. I did not feel any pain at first, but when the feeling in my arm returned it just stung.

While in the Company HQ I heard some moaning and saw shuddering coming from a corner. I went over to see who it was and lo and behold, it was the foul-mouthed Reservist corporal who had made our lives hell at Aldershot. I asked him what the problem was. He replied, '*It's my nerves. They're shot to pieces.*' He had not done anything. I couldn't resist saying, '*Well this* has *sorted the men from the boys.*' He did not reply. I walked out and never saw or heard of him again.

Orders were given to withdraw to La Panne. The others came walking back. Everyone was edgy. Taking all our machine guns and equipment with us, we walked over to where the trucks had been parked, loaded the guns and quietly drove away.

After about eight miles, the convoy stopped at a crossroads on the outskirts of La Panne, and the order was given that all equipment had to be immobilized. The machine guns and other weapons were stripped of vital parts and then run over by the vehicles. The locks of the Vickers were taken with us to be discarded some distance away. In order to seize up the truck engines, they were left running with their hoses cut.

Then we proceeded to La Panne. My five-man gun team stayed together and were still in good order when we reached it. The whole town was under continuous attack from German artillery and bombers. Buildings were on fire and falling into the road. As we were marching along, there were two high-ranking officers in their redcaps standing calmly in the chaos as if they were on the parade ground in Aldershot! One of them was General Alan Brooke. He asked us what our unit was and then said, '*Up the road, and when you get to the end someone will be waiting to guide you, and the Navy will take over to put you in the boats.*' He did not seem at all worried about what was going on around him. He was an inspiration.

The battalion reached the beach. There were men all over the place amongst the tufts of tall grass and soft sand. The battalion remained an organized formation, having worked together as a team, but most of the men there were 'Lines of Communication' troops, and did not have the discipline of the infantry regiments. For them it was probably something new, as they did not normally come under fire and therefore had no idea about what to do.

The Middlesex formed five columns, one per Company including HQ Company. Each column approached the water's edge and was then guided by an officer, who stood there saying, '*Walk in here,*' until it reached our waists. It was not too bad because being at that time of year the water was not overly cold. We still had our own personal weapons, however I managed to slip and drop my rifle in the water. I thought 'Bloody hell, I'm not going to clean that' and left it. Not very soldierly! There were thousands of troops standing in the water, but no sign of boats, large or small could be seen. This was confirmed when, as it became light, word spread along the beach that '*There are no bloody boats.*' We knew it would not be long before the *Luftwaffe* paid us a visit and they did not disappoint. Everyone was still stood there like sitting ducks, with the water now up to our chests, when about half-a-dozen *Messerschmitts* in line abreast came roaring down the beach, machine-gunning and of course there was not a lot we could do. Fortunately, it was only one pass, probably due to the length of the beach.

With the tide coming in, an order came to get back to the beach, so everyone struggled back to the shore in their sodden clothes.

We stayed in the sand dunes for a few hours, being shelled, bombed and machine-gunned at various times. All the boats we could see had been bombed. Finally, an order was given to split into gun crew groups under an NCO and to make our way into Dunkirk, which was on fire about ten miles along the coast. There were all sorts of explosions going on, when an officer from 'B' Company who was leading a line of his blokes he had gathered, said to us, *'Do you want to come with me? I've got my cheque book with me. I'm going to hire a yacht to take us all back to England!'* Reluctantly, we followed on the back of his line. Frank Dollin said to me, *'Let's get rid of this bloody fool'* so we started to drop off the back and let them get further and further ahead.[10] Eventually, I did see the officer look back, but he must have thought 'Let them get on with it.'

Frank led my crew along the beach through the sporadic gunfire and bombing. We seemed to be charmed as none of us was hit while many others fell around us. The soft sand was quite handy as the bombs would bore into it before exploding, thereby dissipating some of the blast.[11] Most of the enemy attention seemed to be concentrated on the jetty and the mole in Dunkirk itself, because the Navy ships could pull alongside them.

I lost track of the time but we had walked a considerable distance and the tide had gone out a mile or two when I spotted some people wading out to a small coaster that was beached and lying on its side near the water's edge. It appeared to be on fire, but someone could be seen on board. We walked out and saw that a couple of fifty-gallon oil drums placed on the deck were the cause of the smoke. In fact, they had cut the tops off and filled the drums with oily waste material to give the impression that the boat was on fire, in the hope of duping

---

10. We saw him when we got back to England, but I don't know whether he hired a yacht or not!
11. There have been a lot of stories told, but I never saw anyone who was drunk or panicking. If there was, I did not see it.

the German bombers into attacking the vast amount of other targets rather than one that appeared to be alight. The English crew said they had an anchor out at sea and when the tide eventually came in, hoped to ratchet off and refloat it. We were told that our group was welcome aboard one at a time, but must not show ourselves on deck. I could not see the name of the boat because at the front, where it would have been, one side was on the sand and the other up in the air, out of view. We boarded the boat and went down the only entrance to the hold via a vertical, iron-rung ladder. It was then a wait for the tide.

In the meantime, four Belgian soldiers arrived and came down to the hold. One of them stood on the bottom step of the ladder so that if anything happened, they would be the first out. One of our blokes went up to him and said, '*Come on, move away from the ladder. If anything happens, we'll all have the same chance.*' If anything had hit us, we would not have had much chance anyway. They refused to move away, which resulted in an altercation. One of the sailors looked down into the hold and asked what the noise was. Realizing what was happening he shouted '*Don't argue with them, throw the bastards over the side.*' The Belgians got the message and amid some cursing at us, moved away from the ladder.

It was certainly a long day. The coaster's job must have been to carry coal because when a bomb or a shell landed close by, it blew coal dust into the air and we all ended up looking like black and white minstrels. We seemed to lay in the hold all day until the tide came in. In the heat I fell into an exhausted sleep and it must have been dark when I vaguely remember the boat swaying. Then someone shook me, saying, '*Come on mate, we're coming into bloody Folkestone.*'

It was 2 June and we were not a pretty sight, being absolutely filthy in our unwashed clothes. Lined up on the jetty were members of the Medical Corps and dozens of middle-aged ladies of the Women's Voluntary Service (WVS) with tea and cakes. The jacket of my battledress had been torn in order to apply the dressing to my wounded shoulder and there was a bit of a bloodstain. A crowd of these well-meaning ladies subsequently descended upon me and began fighting over who was going to take care of the 'wounded hero'. I was in greater danger from them than I had been with the Germans. My gallant machine-gun crew were standing there laughing, so I said, *'Don't bloody laugh, help me!'* They were able to tear me away from the clutches of the WVS, amid much clapping and cheering from the on-looking soldiers. I was thrown into a green carriage of a waiting train of the Southern Railway, my mates still defying the attempts of the ladies to assist.

The train steamed away to safety, passed through London and travelled all night, stopping the next day in Wrexham, North Wales, where we went into the barracks of the Royal Welsh Fusiliers.

Here I went to the medical room, where the doctor just smacked a bit of iodine on my wound and said, *'You're warm. You'll do!'*

*   *   *

The Dunkirk evacuation ended during the night of 3 June. Incredibly, around 330,000 British and 20,000 French troops had been brought back to England.[12]

---

12. My Company Commander, Captain John Panks, was awarded the Military Cross for bravery during the withdrawal to Dunkirk. There were two brothers in the Company and one of them was John Panks' driver. As they were driving along they were shot up by the Germans. The brother was blinded and Panks, who was either brave or stupid, [is there much difference?] shot the Germans and drove his driver back to safety.

Chapter Three

England

Six days later, what was left of the battalion, which of course had arrived back in England piecemeal, began to reassemble at Bridestowe near Okehampton. There we rested, reorganized and were re-kitted with uniforms.

On 13 June the 'Die Hards' were sent to defend the area of Corfe Castle near Swanage. The Germans were expected to make an immediate attempt at invasion and every available man was being employed on coastal defence. This entailed preparing bridges for demolition, organizing roadblocks at strategic points and digging shelter trenches. There was also anti-parachutist guard duty. Close to us was a big hill and at night we would look at it, waiting for parachutists to come over the top. In the darkness you would imagine them. If there was a bit of fluff from the top of a flower, it would be '*Look! There's a parachutist!*'

A week later, the battalion was sent to defend part of an area of the Isle of Wight between Nodes Point and Sandown. 12 Platoon was stationed in a 'strongpoint' right on the beach, this being a wooden beach-hut, lined inside with sandbags. The hut was dilapidated and even the sandbags were split. We were more in danger of being buried alive than attacked. In the end the weight of the sandbags pushed this beach-hut over. Fortunately, everyone slept in houses on the promenade.

There were only a couple of antiquated rifles between us with two clips of bullets, that is ten rounds. When on duty, the rifle had to be handed over, together with the five rounds of ammunition, to the next soldier taking over the guard. I asked whoever was in charge, '*What are you supposed to do when you've fired the five rounds?*' The answer was '*I don't know.*' I said, '*Well I know what I'm going to do, bloody run for it!*'

We never moved around because there was no transport. A few civilian vehicles were requisitioned but that was all.

On 8 July we left the Isle of Wight and travelled to Coggeshall in Essex, coming under the command of the 15th Scottish Division. Daily air raid warnings, although no actual raids, and aerial activity from both sides became the norm.

About ten days later the battalion relieved the 7th Kings Own Scottish Borderers in their coastal defence positions, and 'C' Company went to Tollesbury on the River Blackwater. The weather during this period was miserable, with heavy rain and being quite cold.

Here, we were re-equipped to some extent and stayed there until 5 August, being relieved by the 8th Royal Scots. 'C' Company moved to St Osyth, a few miles west of Clacton on Sea and subsequently, once a week, we had to go into the local Butlin's holiday camp for a bath.

The battalion was temporarily placed in a formation known as The Suffolk Brigade that not surprisingly comprised the three Territorial battalions of the Suffolk Regiment. The 1/7th Middlesex had a lot of replacements so there was a lot of machine-gun training carried out around this time.

August saw an increase in aerial activity and with many foreigners serving in the RAF, everyone was lectured on the uniforms and identification of Polish, Czech, Dutch, Free French and Belgian pilots and ordered that when someone landed by parachute, to check this before deciding which nationality he was! Several German planes were brought down in the sea close to us, although I never actually saw any pilots, but on one occasion a bloke was walking around showing people a German airman's boot. It still had the foot in it. Nothing else had remained.

On Saturday 7 September, all leave was cancelled. During the afternoon, while on guard duty someone said, '*Look at all those bloody seagulls flying in.*' As they got closer it became apparent that they were not seagulls but aeroplanes. It turned out to be the *Luftwaffe's* first major raid on London. They passed over but we could do nothing.

Invasion alert continued to be high during the month as the tides were perfect for it, and so the battalion remained in this area observing RAF patrols and going through air raid warnings up to four times a day.

Over the next month or so, the Battle of Britain gradually petered out and on 21 November most of the battalion, including 'C' Company, moved to Colchester, taking over the Roman Way Camp. Work immediately began on improving the camp defences, particularly sandbagging. A great deal of concentrated training commenced, ranging from Divisional schemes and demonstrations to Company and Platoon exercises, including lectures.

*   *   *

The New Year arrived and brought with it freezing weather and heavy snow. Much of January and February were spent preparing for and taking part in various exercises. Then the battalion moved to take over a new area in Suffolk, relieving the 4th Cheshires and setting up Battalion HQ at Claydon. At this stage, 12 Platoon was commanded by Second Lieutenant Eaves and Sergeant Harry Kingsland.

In May 1941, in order to give us confidence that the gas masks supplied to us actually worked, we had to endure a 'Gas Chamber Test'. Entering a sealed shed, everyone sat around and put the gas masks on. Then someone came in and let loose a gas. We sat there for five minutes then had to take the mask off for a few seconds and walk out. I don't know what kind of gas it was, but it took your breath away and made your eyes water!

During August another move was made, this time to Braiseworth, near Eye, in North Suffolk. A month here was followed by two months at Ipswich, during which time further weapon and specialist training was carried out. Also during this month, our Commanding Officer Lieutenant Colonel Rackham was posted to the 9th Armoured Division. He was eventually replaced by Lieutenant Colonel P.P.C. Tuckey.

On 26 October the battalion moved to Bulford, for a fortnight's concentrated training under the staff of the Small Arms School at Netheravon. We had an instructor from the Staffordshire Regiment called Bissett. He thought he was the cat's whiskers. To obtain a pass you had to be perfectly turned out. On one occasion I had taken particular care in my presentation. I went in to see him and he said, *'What do you want?'* *'I've come for a pass, sergeant.'* He looked at me and said, *'Pass denied. Dismissed.'* I thought 'Why the bloody hell has he said that?' but was not too bothered because you got a pass to go nowhere. There was nothing to do. I started to walk out when he said, *'Come back here.'* I turned around. *'Do you know why I've cancelled your pass?'* *'No, Sergeant Bissett.'* He said, *'You've got idle bootlaces.'* I knew he wasn't joking. He had never joked in his life. *'Go on, off you go.'* So I started to walk out again when he said, *'Come back here!'* *'You don't know what I'm talking about do you?'* *'No, Sergeant Bissett.'* *'Your laces, the two bits are idle. That's a Court Martial offence. They should be pulled together. Go and put yourself right and I'll give you a pass.'* I went back to our Nissen Hut and told the others. They could not believe it. No one had ever heard of it before. The boots were fairly new and a bit tough, so by the time I had sorted myself out, it was too late to get a pass anyway!

The Staffordshire Regiment cap badge was a knot, and whenever the opportunity presented itself, Sergeant Bissett would say to us, *'Where the fighting's hot, you'll find a Staffordshire knot.'* This went on until finally it was too much for someone, and a voice piped up from the back, *'It's a pity you don't bloody join 'em!'*

On 15 November the battalion was transferred to the 51st Highland Division, for whom it was to act as a support battalion, and ordered to move up to Scotland, to Ballater near Aberdeen. We travelled up by truck and upon arrival, as we were driven through the streets, people and some of the Division's soldiers were stopping beside the road watching us coming along. When the convoy stopped for some reason, we were warmly welcomed by one of these Highland soldiers saying,

'*What the bloody hell do you want? We don't want you English up here.*' He got the reply '*We don't want to bloody be here either!*'

Our billet was a big country house. Everything was boarded up to stop it being damaged by the 'riff-raff'. Frank Dollin and I stayed together but there were now three new faces for the other members of my gun crew.

* * *

The 51st Highland Division consisted of three Brigades which each had three battalions:

- 152 Brigade: 2nd Seaforth Highlanders, 5th Seaforth Highlanders, 5th Cameron Highlanders
- 153 Brigade: 5th Black Watch, 1st Gordon Highlanders, 5/7th Gordon Highlanders
- 154 Brigade: 1st Black Watch, 7th Black Watch, 7th Argyll & Sutherland Highlanders

Each Company of the 1/7th Middlesex Battalion was attached to a specific brigade, as follows:

- Battalion HQ was attached to the 51st Highland Division HQ
- 'A' Company, which comprised Numbers 4, 5 and 6 Platoons, were under the command of Divisional HQ
- 'B' Company was 7, 8 and 9 Platoons and attached to 152 Brigade
- 'C' Company was 10, 11 and 12 Platoons, attached to 153 Brigade
- 'D' Company was 13, 14 and 15 Platoons, attached to 154 Brigade

The next few months were spent doing what were called hardening exercises and training schemes. The weather was bitterly cold, and there was of course plenty of snow about. One of these hardening exercises was to take the officers out when they went shooting wildlife such as hares. We would be up and down the mountains, beating the ground to make the hares go in the direction they wanted. That was put down as training.

In late March 1942, the 1/7th Middlesex, having become very fit in Scotland, came down to Mandora Barracks, Aldershot for more extensive training.

The following month Lieutenant Colonel J.W.A. Stephenson assumed command of the battalion.

At the end of April the Army Commander, Lieutenant General Bernard Montgomery, visited the battalion and in the middle of May the Secretary of State for War, Sir James Grigg, and the Commander-in-Chief Home Forces, Lieutenant General B.C.T. Paget, accompanied by the Divisional Commander, Major General Douglas Wimberley, known as 'Big Tam', came to watch the battalion sports, held on Albuhera Day. Ten days later it was the turn of the Adjutant General, Lieutenant General Sir Ronald Adam, who inspected the battalion on parade. On 1 June, their majesties the King and Queen arrived in Aldershot to inspect the 51st Highland Division. The officers always picked out the big fellows for parades like that, and I was bloody glad as well. I was only five foot six tall, plus about half an inch for my ammo boots, but when they came round to choose, just to make sure I would bend my knees to make me even smaller. It avoided all that polishing and not only that, you could go and lay in your barrack room instead.

These visits and inspections were a strong enough indication that the battalion was reaching the end of its training in England.

That same night, 'B', 'C' and 'D' Companies performed a practice night shoot in preparation to fire over the heads of the Division. The following day we carried out the actual shoot over the heads of the entire 51st Highland Division, with ourselves specifically firing over 1st Black Watch and later the 5/7th Gordons.

Five days later, all of the Companies went to the Hog's Back near Guildford for a competitive fire and movement exercise where we were strafed by a Hawker Hurricane, and so got into cover and practiced controlled return fire on the aircraft. Also, one of the things that had to be done was for everyone to be 'run over' by tanks. Tanks of the 5th Canadian Armoured Division, Grants, ran over our trenches that were thirteen feet long by two feet wide by four feet deep, to prove we could stand it. These trenches had been occupied many times before and were worn down somewhat by previous similar exercises. When I heard these tanks approaching, I thought 'God help us'. As one passed over my trench it blew its hot exhaust fumes around me, but then it was away and gone.

Just over a week later a doctor gave everyone a lecture on tropical hygiene. Another lecture, this time on security followed and on 15 June we began tidying the barrack area and packing our kit.

* * *

At 0930 hours on 17 June 1942, the whole battalion was called to the Dining Hall in Mandora Barracks and informed by the CO that we would be leaving that day for the port of embarkation. Everyone filled in a last postcard to their family. All of these would be sent by Mrs Stephenson, the CO's wife, upon receipt of a cable to the effect that the battalion had safely reached its destination.

All of the Highland Division had been issued with tropical kit, which was a slightly lighter and thinner battledress including shorts, plus pith helmets. With this and having had the hygiene lecture, the big rumour was that we were going to India.

Later that night, two trains took the battalion from the Aldershot sidings to Glasgow docks, arriving there at around midday. We immediately boarded a ship, the 23,500-ton former luxury liner, the *Stratheden*.

Approximately 5000 officers and men of the 51st Highland Division HQ, Divisional Troops, 7th Black Watch and various others were on board and it was very crowded. Four troop decks were allocated to the Middlesex. The following day was spent organising ourselves on these decks. Warrant Officers and NCOs were accommodated in cabins on 'D' Deck, while the officers were on 'C' Deck. Everyone was then informed of the ship's routine and practice of the lifeboat drill commenced. We were also instructed not to sit on the ship's rails for fear of falling overboard. As a deterrent it was made clear that the ship would not stop to pick anyone up.

Two days later, the *Stratheden* sailed twenty miles up the Clyde and joined the remainder of the convoy at Gourock. During the afternoon of 21 June the convoy, consisting of twenty-three ships and five destroyers, finally sailed away into the unknown.

Chapter Four

Arrival in the Desert

After five days at sea HMS *Malaya*, a battleship of the Queen Elizabeth class joined the convoy, while HMS *Anaconda* and two destroyers departed.

The weather during this part of the voyage was pretty good, so the Atlantic Ocean was quite calm, much to the relief of many people on board. Everyone slept in hammocks and had to mark their hammock with name and number so the sling position chosen on that first night had to be retained throughout the voyage. Everybody had to sleep 'head to foot', and the hammocks were so close together that they touched each other. When the ship rolled, the whole deck of blokes swayed one way and then the other, just like a lullaby! I learned that if you had to get out in the night to use the toilet, with having to stagger as the ship rolled and all the hammocks swaying, you could never find the way back to your own.

There was not a lot to do apart from physical exercise and lectures. No training could be done on the machine guns as they were all stowed away. The following became the typical routine for a day:

0600 hours – Reveille.
0645 hours – Hammocks rolled and stacked.
0700 hours – Breakfast [first sitting].
0745 hours – Breakfast [second sitting].
0830 hours – Sick parade.
0830 hours – Sweepers parade.
1000 hours – Troop decks clear, except Deck Sergeants, Mess Orderlies, Sanitary parties and Stand-by men in cabins.

1015 hours – Muster parade – all ranks parade on deck under Unit and draft arrangements.

1130 hours – Troops allowed below.

1200 hours – Dinner [first sitting].

1245 hours – Dinner [second sitting].

1300 hours – Sweepers parade.

1600 hours – Tea [first sitting].

1630 hours – Sweepers parade.

1645 hours – Tea [second sitting].

1900 hours – Supper [first sitting].

1945 hours – Supper [second sitting].

2000 hours – Hammocks could be slung from this time onwards.

2100 hours – Sweepers parade.

2200 hours – Lights out. Rounds. All those not on duty to turn in.

2300 hours – Lights out in the saloons.

The food was basic because so many men were crammed on the ship, and dinner was usually stew. A canteen was open from 1145 to 1400 hours, and 1600 to 2000 hours, but there were always such big queues that I never bothered using it.

Fresh water had to be conserved. However, it was available for washing between 0630 and 0700 hours, and 1800 to 1830 hours. Hot and cold salt water were available at all times. Water bottles could be filled on alternate days from the galley. A kettle of water could be drawn by the Mess Orderly of each Mess, for drinking at dinner. Again, this was drawn from the galley.

Due to the U–Boat threat, smoking, the striking of matches or showing lights of any kind was forbidden on open decks during the blackout hours. The throwing of cigarettes overboard was also forbidden. Portholes could not be opened without permission and definitely not during the blackout hours. Everyone had been supplied with a lifebelt that had to be carried at all times unless instructed otherwise.

Regular exercises for such an event or an air attack took place and there were two types of alarm. An intermittent alarm gong was the signal for everyone to go to their enemy attack station, this being for us, our respective deck. The other signal was a continuous alarm gong that indicated that we were to head for our boat station and await further orders, possibly to abandon ship.

The ship sailed by the Azores and then down the west coast of Africa, passing the Cape Verde Islands. After arriving in these warmer waters, porpoises and flying fish followed the ships for days, eating all the stuff that was thrown overboard from the cookhouse. This was done at night to avoid U–Boats spotting the rubbish.

On 2 July, after thirteen days at sea, we laid off Freetown, Sierra Leone, to take on water, fuel and stores. No one was allowed ashore and the normal routine continued. The natives caused some amusement by coming out in their little boats to try and sell us bits and pieces such as fruit, but of course the ship was so high up that business could not be done, probably fortuitously as we might have caught dysentery. It was so hot below deck, and this was only relieved when our allotted time arrived to go on deck for a breath of fresh air. With Divisional HQ being on the ship, every time we went up, the pipers were practising, although without the bags on, just using the chanter, the pipe itself. Even so, we were almost glad to get back down again.

On 6 July the ship sailed again. There was a Middlesex Dance Band that was kept busy and during this period many inter-battalion sports competitions took place such as obstacle races, boxing and tug-of-war.

The 8 July saw General Wimberley give us a lecture on discipline, morale and efficiency. He also mentioned the Middlesex Regiment's fine record in the First World War with only thirty-six men being taken prisoner of war.

Six days later the sea began to get rougher as we neared the Cape of Good Hope, but I was a good sailor and it did not affect me.

A further ten days later, Table Mountain came into view and the convoy split between Cape Town and Durban. Thirteen ships moved towards Cape Town, while the remaining nine, including the *Stratheden* headed for the latter. At this stage the sea got even rougher as some found to their cost, and someone spotted a submarine that turned out to be a whale! Land was sighted again during the early morning of 20 July, and shortly after we docked in Durban Harbour. After twenty–eight days at sea, everyone was allowed ashore until 2300 hours that night.

The following afternoon, everyone formed up on the quayside. We were standing there melting in the heat when a civilian walking by wearing a big heavy overcoat said to us, '*It's cold today isn't it boys?*' We marched off to a transit camp at the P.B.S. Woolsheds, Cargella Road, owned by a Mr Vernon E. Hooper. It was on a racecourse or something similar.

PT and route marches commenced the next morning, but from 1400 hours everyone was let out of the camp. One of our blokes had an aunt who had emigrated to South Africa before the war, and she lived a short distance from the camp, so we paid her a visit. These people made us very welcome, and we spent a lot of our time in her house.

After five days we left the camp and marched back through Durban to the ship and re-embarked. At 0500 hours the following morning, the *Stratheden* moved from the docks into the harbour with two other ships. The Middlesex left six men behind in Durban, five suffering from malaria and one deserter from 'C' Company. The convoy reassembled and then moved off to the east of Madagascar, due to the Japanese submarine threat in the Mozambique Channel. The training, boat drills and lectures started again.

The end of July saw us in the Indian Ocean, around six days sailing from Aden. The convoy was slowly splitting up, going to various destinations, and on 3 August three further ships left for India, confirming that it was not going to be our destination. During the journey there had been nothing but bad news from North Africa, where our forces had fallen back to El Alamein and so there had already been a rumour circulating that they would divert us to Egypt. This certainly now looked like the case.

*   *   *

The 6 August arrived and after forty days at sea, Aden was reached during the afternoon. It was now very hot. However, there was no disembarkation here and the next day the *Stratheden* and two other ships sailed off towards The Red Sea. This was the hardest part of the voyage because it became so hot, with the winds from the Arabian side plus those from Africa. The temperature below decks rose to 114 degrees Fahrenheit.

With the concern about dive-bombing, during the last part of the journey the ship proceeded at full speed. Finally on 11 August 1942, we reached Port Tewfik, at the top of the Red Sea, and were taken off the ship in lighters to Shell Dock. Once ashore everyone was lined up on the jetty waiting to board a train. My first experience of Egypt occurred when a disabled child passed along our line, walking on his knees, begging. An Egyptian policeman came along and started whipping this little boy to try and drive him away. The English blokes were not going to tolerate that and he was told to stop. He responded by jabbering away, so one of them kicked him up the arse. Trucks then took us to a transit camp for the night. The following morning, everyone boarded a train that moved up the west side of the Suez Canal to Quassasin. From Quassasin Station, trucks took us out into the desert to a place called Camp No 18. The area was flat and sandy but featureless apart from the mass of camps. It was soon realized that there were insufficient tents to accommodate the whole battalion, but the Companies began digging sites for their tents anyway, about three feet below the level of the ground. This was apparently because the *Luftwaffe* was liable to come over at night and drop anti-personnel bombs, so it was extra protection. A week was allocated for the battalion to settle in and sort out the stores when they arrived. These subsequently began to arrive from the ship, but there was no sign of the machine guns!

On 17 August rigorous desert training commenced. Due to the heat, the day was split into two periods, with the morning spent out in the desert getting used to the conditions, mainly doing route marches, long carries, and digging slit trenches. There was a siesta during the afternoon. It was just too hot to do anything and the flies were terrible. Further training took place in the camp area from 1730 to 1930 hours. Individuals were trained in the tasks they would carry out in battle, and irrespective of their individual gun numbers, taught to become machine-gunners. The next day was similar but during the night we went out into the desert to practice night navigation.

The hunt for the battalion's missing crates and machine guns went on for another two days. The Divisional area had been searched without success, but they were eventually found in a broken down 3-Ton truck at Tel el Kebir.

On 22 August the Prime Minister, Winston Churchill, inspected the Division. We had to stand along the road because he was coming along it in a car. He was about two hours late and we had all stood there in the sun, slowly melting. Consequently, when he did approach, the order '*Three cheers for Churchill*' was given, but the only people to cheer were the officers! The car just drove straight past. Apparently, while addressing the officers, he reminded them that the 51st Highland Division had many old scores to pay off against the enemy and that '*Your time may not be long delayed.*'

*   *   *

The poverty and conditions of the locals was shocking. They lived in hovels. There were open drains with sewage floating down the side of the street. The Sweet Water Canal ran from Port Said to Suez, and why they ever called it that I do not know. There was everything floating in it, including dead donkeys.

We had been warned about various things that should not be done, one of them being not to eat anything soft-skinned: '*Water Melons. It is reported that native vendors of water melons, resort to the expedient of pumping up melons with water from the Sweet Water Canal in order to make their produce look juicier and more attractive. To eat such produce is highly dangerous to the health, and all ranks will therefore not purchase water melons from native vendors. Only water melons issued in rations will be eaten.*'

Of course we thought we knew better. At breakfast time the Arabs would come around selling '*Hot, sweet tea. Hot, sweet tea! Eggs-a-bread. Egg-a-bread!*' We bought some melons from them and within a few hours were suffering from terrible dysentery, ending up in a tented hospital set up for just such cases. You did not have much 'warning' from what we were suffering, so all sides of the tents were rolled up for a quick escape!

The sister in charge of this hospital was married to a chap in the RAF out there. His squadron had twin-engined Boston bombers and she knew what was going on, because every time they returned from a raid, no matter what she was doing, she would rush outside and count them.

*   *   *

After a couple of painful weeks I was discharged. Three days later the 1/7th Middlesex moved forward to Cowley Camp in the area west of Cairo. About five miles away the pyramids and Sphinx could be seen, although I did not get the chance to visit them, but then it was too hot to do anything.

Ever since the *Afrika Korps* had been halted at El Alamein, the next move of its commander, General Erwin Rommel, had been awaited. Then suddenly the whole of the HD was placed at two hours notice, with its main commitment being the defence of Cairo in case Rommel by-passed our main defences and headed straight for the city. 'A' and 'D' Companies were assigned to defend the el Mulut Canal and so took up defensive positions, holding five crossings and the approaches to the bridges. 'B' Company had the Delta Barrage and 'C' Company, the outer zone of the el Giza–Mena Canal. 12 Platoon was assigned to 152 Brigade. We continued to dig in over the next two days and the rest of 'C' Company joined us within 152 Brigade. The particular platoon commanded by Lieutenant MacPherson actually had its positions situated near the Sphinx. Everyone was put on two hours notice to take up battle positions, as evidence that Rommel was to make his attack became apparent.

On 31 August Rommel made his attempt to breach the Alamein 'Line'. However, General Montgomery had taken over command of the Eighth Army and knew exactly what he was doing. The Germans and Italians were forced to pass what was called the Ruwiesat Ridge and when they had moved all their tanks and transports below that ridge, he trapped them and they were hammered with artillery and tank fire. The various battles went on for a few days, but the Axis Forces achieved little and were forced to retire.

On 9 September, with Cairo now free from immediate danger, the Highland Division was ordered to move forward to an area known as the 'second line of defence'. This entailed a two-day journey through the desert to what were known as fortified boxes. There was no continuous front line in the desert, but there were a number of these fortified boxes positioned around the area that supported each other. These were surrounded by barbed wire and extensive minefields, which isolated the boxes and denied the ground in between. Access was gained through marked gaps in the minefields. Each box comprised a Brigade of infantry with all supporting arms, machine guns, anti-tank guns, artillery and mortars, and was self-supporting for a week in food, water and ammunition. The route to our box was along a well-worn track that was covered in a thick, fine powdery dust. As we drove along, those in the leading vehicles were not troubled too much by it because of course most of the dust went behind them, but especially with our 15cwt Morris Commercials being further back, we suffered. The only thing you could do was to turn your back. The drivers were fine as they had goggles that completely covered both eyes. When the battalion arrived during the late evening of the second day, it looked like a ghostly army, with every man and vehicle being covered from head to foot by this grey dust.

'C' Company had been moved back to 153 Brigade, and our particular box was situated twenty-five miles east of El Alamein.

The Division was here for the express reason of training. During the day, the main thing to do was to just not move. No one was allowed to drink from his water bottle. That was used as the last resort and could only be drunk when ordered to do so. Each water bottle was regularly inspected to make sure it was still full. I think they held about two pints. When water was brought up, we were never issued with it. Each man was entitled to two pints a day, but if it had been distributed individually, some blokes would be inclined to drink theirs quickly and ask for some of yours later. Therefore, we had all agreed that the platoon cook would have it, as he could use it to better advantage. He could make tea. The cook would be further back, just behind the guns.

There was no twilight as such. The sun went down very quickly and at night it became freezing cold, and very dark. It was so black at night that while in this box, due to the surrounding minefields, if someone had to go to the next sentry post or trench, we were told '*If you get lost, don't wander about. Just sit down and wait where you are until it gets light.*' On one occasion, I was out with another bloke and we did get lost, and so sat on the ground all night. When the first vestiges of light became apparent, we could have almost touched where we had wanted to go![1]

Food-wise, everything was tinned. The Army lived on bully beef stew. The worst thing though was the flies, millions of them. At one stage an order was issued for every man to kill fifty flies a day, after which they were burned. There was also a particular kind of bird. I do not know what its name was but we called them 'shitehawks'. They were like dive-bombers. You could go to the cookhouse, get your grub in a mess tin and they would come straight down and take it out of your bloody hand.

* * *

During 1941, the Australian 9th Infantry Division had been the garrison of the surrounded and beleaguered Tobruk. The location

---

1. It was here that we sustained our first casualty. One morning a Corporal Nutt was found dead after being shot in the head. No one knew what had happened. He had only just got married before leaving England.

had a profusion of deep caves and many of the Aussies lived in them, providing safety from the virtual non-stop bombing and shelling. Before attacking, Rommel had told his men '*They are living like rats in holes, and we are going to dig them out.*' The Aussies held fast and the name 'Desert Rat' stuck and was adopted as the emblem of the 7th Armoured Division. In fact the emblem is not a rat at all, but a rodent of the desert called a Jerboa. Rommel also called the Aussies '*The ten thousand thieves*', a reference to their ancestors at Botany Bay. Instead of being insulted, the Aussies thought it hilarious.

* * *

On 17 September certain 'Die Hards' were sent to the 2/28th Infantry Battalion MG, 9th Australian Division for combat experience. They were holding a five-mile area of the front line, west of Alamein. I was with a rather youthful looking Lieutenant called Alan Carter. He had big, rimmed glasses and looked like a schoolboy, but he was all right. His looks gave the wrong impression of his capabilities. He had been brought up in a very posh school and so was very polite and talked nicely. I wasn't much better, because I also looked young. When we reached the forward position a Corporal said, '*What the hell are you doing here?*' Alan introduced us and the Aussie said '*You had better come and see my sergeant.*' So we were taken to the dugout of their platoon commander, a veteran sergeant, where our guide introduced us. '*Here Charlie, look what the f*****g cat's dragged in.*' He looked us up and down in disbelief before saying to Alan, '*Does your mummy let you drink beer?*' '*Oh yes, Sergeant!*' He then gave us a bottle each and said, '*Stick that in your mouth!*'

After explaining why we were there, the sergeant said, '*I'll give you two passes to go to Alexandria for the week instead of staying here. We won't tell anyone!*' Alan said, '*We'd better see something as they'll ask us what we've done when we get back.*' We were the prize showpiece amongst these Aussies. They all came to have a look at us. '*Bloody hell, are they all like you back in England?*' They were all right afterwards.

The Aussies readily passed on their expertise of fighting in the desert to us. They called their slit trenches 'Douvres'.[2] These trenches were big enough for two men and whenever possible, were covered with corrugated iron sheets, which in turn were covered with sand. The sheets were carried on their 15cwt trucks.

We also learned about digging 'V' shaped trenches whenever possible, with the Vickers gun inside the 'V', pointing away from the apex. This allowed you to walk around the trench and give a ninety-degree field of fire. Each arm of the 'V' was about six feet long and only shoulder-wide to reduce the chance of being hit by shrapnel. It also allowed the gun crew Numbers 1 and 2 to sleep with their legs out and backs to the wall. This would be at least three feet deep, depending on what was being dug out. The higher numbers in the crew, responsible for fetching the belts up, would dig their two-man trenches behind us. They were staggered back so that one shell burst would only affect one trench. In theory, if we had a Number 4, which we never did because there were never enough men, he would take the metal containers containing the ammunition up to the Number 3's trench, he would then take it up to the Number 2 at the gun position.

*   *   *

In October, after we returned to our unit, the Highland Division started practicing for the coming attack at El Alamein with various exercises. Also, two practice night attacks took place in a spot in the desert that was similar to where the Alamein attack would go in. This practice was the first time we had to fire live ammunition over the advancing infantry in the desert. Sandbags were placed under the barrel just in case the tripod legs should sink into the sand. The Jocks moving through us said, '*You're not gonna shoot that bloody thing over us are you?*' '*I'm afraid so.*' '*Bloody hell.*'

---

2. That is why the 5th Black Watch Club is called 'The Douvre Club'.

Away from the coast the desert was featureless, and so an objective such as a village or town could not be stipulated. Consequently, all directions had to be taken by compass, but even then a truck could affect magnetic north. We would be advancing on foot and under an artillery barrage, so the method was that the navigator followed a specified bearing at so many paces per minute for a certain number of minutes. Then there would be a change of direction and perhaps walk at a slower or quicker pace, so many paces again on your new direction for ten minutes and so on, zig-zagging across the desert. According to the timetable, the speed walked and the direction taken, the artillery knew where you were or should be. In practice, this did not always turn out to be correct.

The 51st Highland Division was positioned between the 9th Australian Division on our right and the 2nd New Zealand Division to our left, with the 1st South African Division beyond them. The HD itself was set up with 154 Brigade in the north and 153 Brigade to the south. 152 Brigade was in reserve. The battalions were placed from north to south as follows; the 5th Black Watch, 5/7th Gordon Highlanders, 1st Black Watch, 7th Argyll and Sutherland Highlanders, and finally two companies of the 5th Cameron Highlanders. Each would be spread over a frontage of around 600 yards to a depth of similar distance. 12 Platoon of the Middlesex, now under the command of a new and competent Platoon Commander, Lieutenant Humphrey Wigan, was attached to 5/7th Gordon Highlanders. Our proposed route of advance was to be through some of the heaviest enemy defences.

Before an attack a certain number of men were left behind so that there was a residue to form a new battalion. These were called LOBs, 'Left out of Battle' and all our personal kit that could not be carried was passed to them to be looked after.

During the night before the attack, we moved forward so that there was not so far to walk to the Start Line, which was a few miles from the German position and several hundred yards beyond our own minefield. Our trenches, which were east of the El Alamein railway station, had already been dug, so we just got into them and made ourselves comfortable. The 15cwt trucks brought all the guns forward, then turned around and went back. The orders were not to get out or show ourselves and so the next day, 23 October, everyone stayed in the trenches, awaiting the start of the barrage. We had water, plus five days rations.

∗   ∗   ∗

Our own immediate plan was for infantry and engineers to clear gaps through the enemy minefields. The Gordons were then to advance to reach four lines in turn, named Green, Red, Black and Blue at ever increasing distances from the Start Line, but in strict timing with the artillery barrage. The infantry was therefore to keep up close behind the barrage. Then at first light, tanks of the 1st Armoured Division would pass through them. Of course, spread in between all of these coloured lines over four miles were German and Italian machine-gun outposts and other stronger defensive positions possessing anti-tank guns that had to be overcome. All such known defensive positions had been given names of Scottish mountains, towns or landmarks. The Gordons had detailed eight officers and NCOs to guide us with their compasses.[3]

The exercises had shown that the infantry advanced far too quickly for the support troops like us when we had to carry all the necessary equipment, plus our casualties would be far higher. Consequently our role was to arrive after a certain objective had been captured and provide machine-gun support to consolidate the position. However, if they ran into something that could not be dealt with using infantry weapons and needed something heavier, they would send for us.

The whole Division had received a final message from General Wimberley which was as follows: '*As being in the proud position of*

---

3. Before the night was over, seven of these men had been killed or wounded.

Commander of the Highland Division of Scotland, I know I am expressing for all of us what every Scotsman feels in his heart today. Scotland for ever and second to none.' He tactfully added for the Englishmen in the Division, *'A special message for our 'Die Hards'. 'For ever England.'*

Chapter Five

The Second Battle of Alamein

At 2140 hours on 23 October 1942, the sky lit up when over 800 artillery pieces opened fire, carrying out counter-battery work. The spectacle and noise were unbelievable. For the attack we had to carry our equipment. The Number 1 carried the tripod in the prescribed manner while the Number 2 had the Vickers Gun across his shoulders. The remaining Numbers carried the ammunition, two metal boxes in each hand. On top of this, everyone had a pickaxe or a shovel plus four days rations and personal kit. I was also carrying four boxes and a small pack on my back. As I had my hands full, they shoved a pick between the small pack and my back, with the handle down the back of my neck. With the platoon more or less in one line, twenty minutes later, on hearing the skirl of the bagpipes ahead, the pipers were always out in front, we staggered off and moved through prepared gaps in our minefield that were marked by small lights on the ground. These gaps were wide enough for the tanks that would come later.

The Start Line, marked by a tape, was reached and we followed on after the leading Company of the Gordons.

Before long the enemy artillery started answering and the shrapnel began to cause a lot of casualties. The wounded were coming back through us, or just lying where they fell. With the cordite hanging close to the ground and the sand that the shells blew into the air, visibility was almost nil. All you could do was follow the bloke in front, and he followed the man in front of him. If you lost the man in front, you were in trouble, and so were those behind you. Every time I took cover by kneeling or falling to the ground, the bloody pickaxe hit me in the back of the neck, so I decided to 'lose' it. A great big bloke called Charlie Rutt was walking behind me and I got him to pull it out and throw it away. It was even worse for the poor Number 1s, who could not get down at all because the tripod would hit the back of the neck, plus with its weight being over 50lbs they would never get up. The Germans were firing on fixed lines, but fortunately my platoon seemed to be between two of these lines, as shells were bursting on either side of our compass bearing. If we had been a couple of hundred yards in either direction, the platoon would have been decimated.

On we went and suddenly Charlie, who I think was a bit bomb happy, said to me, '*Here, I've been hit!*' A piece of shrapnel had gone up the back of his hand, so I applied his First-Aid dressing and he said, '*I don't want to get gangrene.*' As I thought he was not going to be much good anyway, I said, '*You had better go back, find a First-Aid bloke and get it seen to,*' and off he went. I never saw him again.

Bringing up the rear was Sergeant Harry Kingsland. Nobody liked him, but that night he kept us going with his shouting and swearing. Gradually, some of our men became casualties and they could no longer carry their ammunition boxes, plus after walking with these loads for quite some distance, some started to throw them away. He was shouting, '*Don't throw that ammunition away, we'll need it later!*' With him was our runner, another Charlie, and somehow they had a found a piece of wood. Every time someone dropped an ammunition box, Kingsland would pick it up, pass the wood through the handle, and between the two of them, lift the wood onto their shoulders. In the end, they had about eight boxes of ammunition swinging about, and were staggering along like Donald Duck. He still had enough puff to carry on shouting at us though.

There were quite a few pauses while the Gordons cleared out various positions, and by midnight we had passed a strongpoint called *Cruden*. The resistance mostly consisted of Italians, with a few Germans to 'stiffen them up'. A quarter of a mile further on, the Green Line was reached where an hour was allowed for reorganisation. During this initial phase we had run into an unmarked minefield and this had upset the timing of the operation, but the advance was resumed and after 4,500 yards the Red Line was reached, which was the area of the forward enemy positions. The Gordons then proceeded to advance towards the Black Line. The four Companies of the 5/7th Gordons had suffered heavily from the artillery fire and subsequently mortar and *Spandau* machine-gun fire. They were brought to a halt before the Black Line by two strongpoints codenamed *Strichen* and *Keith* that defended a wide, deep minefield. An attempt was made to outflank it, only to run into another minefield covered by machine guns. As the first signs of daylight appeared, we were still staggering along, but having advanced about three and a half miles from our Start Line we had to stop. Our objective, the Blue Line, was still another mile away.

Just to the north, a strongpoint called *Kintore* and a minefield there held up the advance. By 0740 hours, although we did not know it, 12 Platoon had strayed a few hundred yards north into this area, which was the responsibility of the 5th Black Watch and 1st Gordon Highlanders. A couple of hundred yards in front of us we could hear a lot of shouting in Italian. We were about to come face to face with Mussolini's 'Fascist Legions' who had in 1936, 'bravely' dropped mustard gas bombs on the defenceless Abyssinians. The Italians were actually the first enemy troops we had seen during the night. The Jocks had obviously engaged them but they were the first we had encountered. Many Gordons came from Glasgow, not normally people you would want to annoy, but after this advance they were very upset and someone was going to pay for it. The four Vickers guns were mounted and each fired 500 rounds at these 'I-ties'. Then with fixed bayonets, the Jocks moved forward and worked their frustration out on them. The fight was a short one and I did not see many returning prisoners.

When it became light, we found ourselves located in front of a defensive position known as *Aberdeen*, and between two minefields, one ours, the other German. We attempted to dig ourselves in, but the ground was very stony and the folly of discarding my pickaxe then became apparent. The desert in that area was a layer of sand about twelve inches deep, followed by solid rock. Generally, it was very rocky.[1]

All we could do was to build what was known as a 'Sanger', a word I believe the South African troops had introduced. Each man carried a couple of empty sandbags and these were filled and used to construct a small parapet. Then the sand would be dug out for however deep it would go. Any stones found were put around the outside of the hole. The sand was then scooped against the outside and by lying full length you were just about below the level of the desert. Then you just hoped for the best. When it became necessary to fire, you had to get up and expose yourself. Using the clamps on the tripod, I always set it at the lowest height so that you could get down behind the gun, kidding myself it was a bit safer.

Not long after we had finished digging in, literally dozens of Sherman tanks of the 2nd Armoured Brigade appeared a few hundred yards behind us and stopped, unable to get through the minefield due to the lack of cleared gaps. After a little while the *Luftwaffe* made an appearance and started to drop bombs indiscriminately. I could hear the bombs exploding but one in particular made an almighty clang when it went up, which I can only assume was a direct hit on one of our tanks. Then to our horror, tanks of the 15th Panzer and Italian *Littorio* Divisions appeared from behind the ridge in front of us, about two miles away. They advanced with the sun at their backs and the opposing armoured forces proceeded to open fire. We were stuck in the middle with the solid shot armour-piercing shells passing about six feet above our heads. Not a pleasant position. As this battle went on there was a sudden, strange 'WHOOSH' that was very close. I looked up and saw a spent armour-piercing shell sticking out of a sand bag on my gun pit. Frank Dollin, who knew no fear, pulled it out, walked

1. In fact, the defensive trenches at Alamein had had to be dug out with pneumatic drills. To the south nearer the Quattara Depression it was very sandy. It was impassable to wheeled traffic, so no one had bothered to put any troops down there.

a few yards and threw it away. After several hours, with tanks burning on both sides, the firing died down. It turned out to be a rather an uncomfortable day.

Overall, the initial assault had advanced about five miles, on a front of around six miles, and the New Zealanders had captured the important Miteirya Ridge.

That night of 24/25 we went forward again, to the north of the Kidney feature, and as it became light we opened fire on some Italians. Quite a few of them surrendered but they were not very soldierly. Some came out to surrender with their suitcases already packed! Not long after, during another action, one of the Jocks brought back a member of the *Afrika Korps*, a big strapping German about six feet tall. He was strolling through all these shells and God knows what else and as he passed by, with his coat folded neatly over his arm, he was picking his teeth with a toothpick! I think it was all bravado, but I thought 'I hope they're not all like him!' Thankfully, they were not all like him.

By 2100 hours that night we were sitting on *Aberdeen* itself, which was on the Blue Line, the final objective for the first night. At this point the 5/7th Gordons were withdrawn and replaced by the Seaforths, but we remained in place to support them.

The following day, *Stukas* were concentrating on something beyond a ridge in front of us. They would dive on the target and go out of sight, re-emerging from behind the ridge. After a while we noticed that they re-appeared from behind the ridge at exactly the same place each time. We had all acquired German rifles and ammunition that contained tracer rounds, and so these weapons were used to open fire on them just as they re-appeared. We thought that perhaps one was hit in the tail, although it did not come down, but at least we had the satisfaction of firing at them with their own guns.

On the night of Monday 26 October we pushed forward again. When it became light, it was realized that we had been able to advance further than the troops to our left and right. The maps that we had to rely on were not accurate and with the area being featureless anyway, one sand dune was the same as the next, we had to stay where we were. However, the situation very quickly became desperate, as it was apparent that we were cut off with little food or water and were also very low on ammunition. To make matters worse, the wireless had been knocked out. During this night advance Lance Corporal Herbert 'Sam' Sleeth, our platoon runner, an old reservist bloke with a broad northern accent, had been hit in the back by a piece of shell casing which knocked him off his feet. At the time he was carrying four belts of ammunition, that is a thousand rounds and a case of spare parts. In spite of his wounds he continued for another two miles and although being hit a second time and a third time, still managed to deliver his load to us. The next day our own artillery started firing at us due to the difficulty in pinpointing a location in the desert. Sleeth volunteered to go back over the shell-swept ground to inform them that they were shooting at us and ask for help.

By the next morning there was no water left. We had drunk that held in our water bottles. Never mind the regulations, we never knew if we were going to be alive the next day. Everyone was thirsty. Suddenly to our disbelief a 15cwt truck came up from behind, but went right through our position. It had obviously got lost. Jerry was not too far away and a machine gun opened up, killing the blokes and bringing it to a halt in front and about fifty yards to the right of us. The truck had an open back and we could clearly see the two-gallon water cans on board. Sergeant Kingsland started shouting, '*No one's to go out to that water. No one's to touch it. After dark, we'll have it for the platoon.*' So of course we had to sit there all day looking at these water cans. When it got dark, we saw Kingsland and his runner creeping out there. They reached the truck and Kingsland got in the back. He got hold of one of the metal water containers and went to pass it out to the runner, but it struck the back of the truck with an almighty 'CLANG'. Of course, Jerry had the truck lined up, *Spandau* at the ready. There was a short, very rapid burst of fire and Kingsland fell out the back with a bullet wound to the leg. He was carried away on a stretcher. The

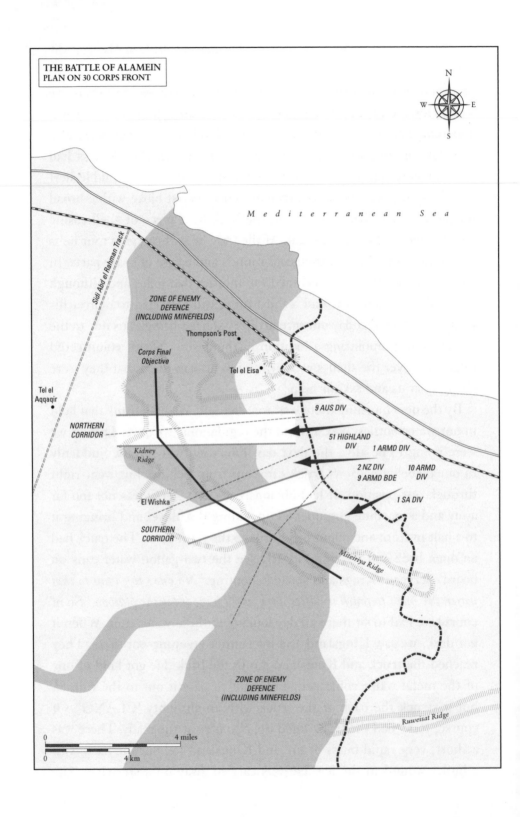

THE BATTLE OF ALAMEIN
PLAN ON 30 CORPS FRONT

N
W E
S

Mediterranean Sea

Sidi Abd el Rahman Track

ZONE OF ENEMY
DEFENCE
(INCLUDING MINEFIELDS)

Thompson's Post

Corps Final
Objective

Tel el Eisa

Tel el
Aqqaqir

9 AUS DIV

NORTHERN
CORRIDOR

Kidney
Ridge

51 HIGHLAND
DIV   1 ARMD DIV

2 NZ DIV   10 ARMD
9 ARMD BDE   DIV

El Wishka

1 SA DIV

SOUTHERN
CORRIDOR

Miteiriya Ridge

ZONE OF ENEMY
DEFENCE
(INCLUDING MINEFIELDS)

Ruweisat Ridge

0   4 miles

0   4 km

runner was all right because he had had the vehicle between himself and the machine gun. Although they did not retrieve any of the water, we did end up getting it, but a lot more surreptitiously than that!

In the meantime, Sam Sleeth had duly arrived at Company HQ and insisted on leading our Company Commander, Major De Monk, back to us with all the necessary supplies. Sleeth only gave in when wounded a fourth time.[2,3]

*   *   *

The following day, the Kidney feature was taken and held against the Axis counter-attacks, particularly during the early morning. We regained contact with the Company.

The positions taken by the HD were consolidated and between the 29 and 31 October further attacks and counter-attacks were made, but little or no progress was made.

It continued to be terrifically hot, especially at midday. I actually saw tanks crews cracking eggs and frying them on the outside of their tanks. Due to the heat, the fighting would start at dawn and by mutual agreement, from about eleven o'clock, it stopped. Neither side could see anything anyway because of the heat haze. Everything shimmered. This period was just spent trying to keep out of the sun. The less you moved about, the less dehydrated you became, so everyone would just lie there and stink. Then when it cooled down, at around three or four o'clock in the afternoon, the war recommenced and went on through the night, when it was much cooler.

All of 12 Platoon had been forced to leave our small packs with the 1st Gordons before the move to the *Aberdeen* strongpoint and they had not been seen since, so the RQMS brought replacements. All our soap

---

2. For this, he was rightfully awarded the Distinguished Conduct Medal. He was later severely wounded at Tomasof in 1945 in the Reichswald.
3. Major De Monk, who was awarded the Military Cross, was later killed as a Lieutenant Colonel leading an infantry battalion in Italy.

had been left behind and consequently we had not had any chance for a wash and shave for two days.

With all the different armies, there were thousands of men in that area, and so our hygiene was very strict. If you had to go, then if possible, you moved fifty yards from the nearest occupied place, dig a hole, do your business, and then cover it up, otherwise there would have been so much disease. Both the British and the Germans were meticulous in doing that, but the Italians were disgusting. They were so frightened they would just go in the end of their trench. This was discovered during an earlier action, when one of our blokes jumped in one, and did not come out smelling of roses. The Arabs would just drop their trousers where they were, wipe their backside with their hand, then wipe it on the sand and think nothing of it!

The Germans also fought in accordance with the rules of the Geneva Convention. They were pretty good. The wounded could always be picked up and they would not shoot at an ambulance. We did the same but the Italians could not be trusted.

* * *

At this time, while returning from liaison with 9 Platoon, my friend Lieutenant Alan Carter of 'A' Company had been badly wounded in the stomach by shrapnel and was picked up by stretcher-bearers of the New Zealand Division. We all wore the same desert uniform and they thought he was one of theirs. Apparently, he spent a week in one of their hospitals before they realized he was a Middlesex man. The Divisional Padre explained that he had seen him and that he was well and cheerful.

* * *

Although from our point of view we did not seem to be getting anywhere, the battle plan must have been working because we moved forward a little every day and every night. The tactical situation had begun to change on the night of 28/29 October. A few days earlier the

Australians had attacked a vital enemy location south of the railway line known as Thompson's Post [the official Arab name was Tel-el-Eisa]. Heavy fighting had ensued but some success was gained. However, their losses were high. The following night the attack continued and carried on across the railway to a paved road. The position was one of extreme importance to the enemy, and on 1 November Rommel subsequently ordered four attacks to try and retake it. The fighting became brutal, but the Australians held on. Following these setbacks, plus the general situation regarding his forces and their supplies, Rommel began to plan the retreat of his forces.

Chapter Six

The Breakout

At 0125 hours on 2 November, the Vickers guns of 'A' and 'C' Companies opened fire for a harassing shoot. Fifteen thousand rounds were fired on a front of 4,000 yards. The indomitable New Zealanders attacked and broke through. That evening, orders were received to advance and in twenty minutes we had moved 1,500 yards without casualties and taken over a hundred Italian prisoners. Later that night it became obvious that the Axis forces were now retreating and another attack went in, but the Company trucks had got lost on their way up to the line and had still not arrived by the time we were due to advance, and so transport was borrowed from 'A' Company.

There was a lot of confusion at this stage with the map reading and coordination of infantry and armour, but the enemy withdrawal turned into full-scale retreat during the late afternoon of 4 November. Many Italians were abandoned and so more prisoners were being taken and by the end of the day the figure was over 2,000 for the Divisional front. Costly attacks, particularly by the 5/7th Gordon Highlanders and the 7th Argylls had opened up the route for the Armoured Divisions. However, there was a route across the desert known as the Rahman Track along which German 88mm anti-tank guns were dug in, and our tanks could not get across it. The German tanks withdrew and the 2nd Armoured Brigade charged after them, straight into these anti-tank guns.[1]

---

1. The Germans used the 88mm very successfully as an anti-tank gun. It was so notorious to the tank regiments that after the war, if Bingo was being played in a British Legion Club, when '88' was called, the shout would always go up, '*Driver reverse!*'

Early the next day, we were ordered to move off towards an enemy airfield to the south of a place called El Daba, thirty miles beyond El Alamein. We duly reached it, but the site was not a proper airfield, more of an airstrip. There were a few temporary buildings and a lot of destroyed German and Italian aircraft strewn around the place.

By this stage 'C' Company was not strong enough to continue the pursuit of the Axis Forces as we had suffered many casualties and needed to be reinforced. Also transport-wise, the Company now only possessed one jeep, two 30 cwt or 2.5 Ton trucks, ten 15 cwts, one water cart and one captured vehicle. And so this halt gave us the chance for a rest and logistic build up before moving forward across the desert.

One of the first things we had to have was a hair inspection! Everyone's was found to be too long due to the lack of hair cutting equipment.

For the next two days it rained non-stop, turning everything into a sea of sand. The Axis Forces were retreating along the only road, which ran along the coast towards Sollum. The 7th Armoured Division was in pursuit up this road, but had been slowed by the Germans blowing craters in it or planting mines, and now this rain further hampered them.

While at El Daba we received a message from General Wimberley, which was forwarded to the whole of the Highland Division:

'Now that we have finished the first phase of our fighting, I want to write you a short line to congratulate you on the magnificent fighting carried out by your Division. You have had a tremendous reputation to live up to and you have fought side by side with highly experienced and trained Divisions. It speaks volumes to the credit of your Division that they have held their own magnificently with the Divisions and on all occasions achieved their objectives.

The spirit of your men has been magnificent and I hope you will convey to them my intense appreciation and admiration of what they have done.

We now set forth on a new venture and ahead of us lie many difficult tasks. We shall have to train and work hard for the roles that lie ahead. I am very proud that your Division is to continue in the Corps and I look forward to our future fighting with complete confidence.

In the last fourteen days, we of the 1942 edition, have I am sure, reminded Scotland that we too were chipped off just the same block of northern granite that provided the best British fighting Division of the last Great War.'

*   *   *

On 12 November a conference was held at Divisional HQ to discuss recent operations. One of the matters that arose was the siting of the machine guns, anti-tank guns and infantry once a position had been captured. It was always stressed that the anti-tank guns had priority in choice of position, then the machine guns and then the infantry. However, as the infantry were always out in front and arrived at a location first, they chose their positions and so generally the guns had to fit in around them, finding the best position available. We had encountered this problem on a number of occasions.

On the same day 153 Brigade began to head west. However, we could not move into the desert because the sand was still too soft and with the coastal road having been churned up by the vehicles of both sides, our 15cwt trucks sank up to their axles. These were extracted using what were known as 'sand shoes' for which every vehicle had two fixed to the side. They were metallic and about eighteen inches wide by eight feet long and full of holes. The process was to dig out the front wheels. Then the sand shoes were placed in front of the rear wheels, which would grip on them and begin to move. Before the wheel reached the end of the shoe, another had to placed forward of the front wheel and this carried on until a more solid piece of ground was encountered.

As soon as things had dried up, and it did not take long, everyone got moving and reached El Fuka, another deserted German airstrip close to the coast around sixty miles west of El Alamein, again littered solely with destroyed aircraft.

The 16 November saw us fifty miles further west at Sidi Haneish, where the whole battalion concentrated. The desert was different here to what had previously been encountered because it became very stony.

On 19 November 'C' Company left with 153 Brigade for Tobruk. Travelling along the main road via Sidi Barrani, we crossed into Libya, where the road became known as the *Via Balbo* [Via means road or street], which continued to run along the coast and stretched the length of what had been Italian Libya, from Tripoli, via Sirte, El Agheila, Benghazi, Gazala, and Tobruk, which we reached two days later. The town had been taken eight days previously. Generally, we avoided going into the towns because they were places that stank. They had no sewers or anything like that. Consequently, there was a lot of disease.

By 23 November the Company had moved to an area sixteen miles west of Tobruk. The desert at this point consisted of stretches of saltpans, which because of the time of year were dry, and an escarpement that stretches in the shape of a half-circle to the north, with patches of vegetation and stony ground.

At night, after driving through the desert, the vehicles would always drop us off with the guns, ammunition, equipment and rations we were going to need and then go back to Company Headquarters, which would be as far back as to be at least out of sight. Generally at night, there would be a fifty per cent Stand To, while the remainder had a rest before the changeover.

If possible a hot meal would be brought up in 'dixies', insulated boxes to keep it hot. Sometimes, our old Quartermaster would bring our food up. We'd say, *'Hello Sandy'* and he would get irate. *'Don't you call me Sandy. It's Quartermaster Sergeant to you.'* *'Oh, clear off Sandy!'* And later he did. It was much safer back at HQ and he could not get back there quick enough! There were quite a few sand dunes, so they could park behind them and set up their camouflage nets. We did not want them parked near us anyway, because if they were spotted, Jerry would to try to shell them, and us as well.

The only food available during the day was bully beef and biscuits. Nothing else would keep in the heat. Even then the bully beef would be melted. When a tin was opened, all the grease from the fat would come surging out, but it didn't taste too bad when you were hungry. There was also M & V, meat and veg. God knows what meat it was. The Germans had tinned meat with the initials 'AM' marked on it. The prisoners would swear to us that it was made from '*Alte Manne*', old men, German pensioners! The funny thing was, they liked to eat our bully beef and we liked their tinned meat! Anything for a change I suppose.[2]

*   *   *

From west of Tobruk the Company cut south across the desert with the 5/7th Gordons, through Bir Hacheim, the site of the gallant defence by the 1st Free French Division during the previous May and June.

By 1 December, we were north east of Antelat. This area was one of rolling hills, saltbush and scrub. Here, the water ration was increased to half a gallon a man per day due to there being more Birs in the area. The next day, during the afternoon 12 Platoon passed through the war-torn white houses of Agedabia, having approached it from the north-east. Mersa Brega was a few miles ahead and we were told to keep well dispersed, about 200 yards apart because the RAF had not yet managed to catch up and there was a real danger of the *Luftwaffe* bombing us.

From Alamein the Germans had fallen back 650 miles to prepared positions at El Agheila, which was now less than ten miles away. After

2. For some reason the water from the wells, which the Arabs called *Birs*, tasted odd. The Germans accused us of poisoning it, we accused them and it was not until after the war that it was realized that neither side had done so. It was due to the oil in Libya, seeping through into the wells.

reaching the coast at Mersa Brega, the enemy in front of us began to withdraw again, being forced by an outflanking inland sweep by the New Zealanders. The Germans left behind booby traps and thousands of mines. Orders came down not to enter the town.

Here we suffered a sandstorm. It could be seen approaching, almost like a curtain. All you could do was sit in your slit trench covered by a waterproof cape, turn your back and wait for it to blow over.

El Agheila was around 450 miles from Tripoli, with Alexandria about 700 miles to the east (with only the damaged Tobruk in between), and so it was roughly the end of either side's supply line. Both armies could only maintain small forces there, at the most a Division. The place was littered with knocked out tanks and vehicles from previous fighting.

'C' Company had continued to move with 153 Brigade and was far in advance of the battalion itself. We came to a halt in the area of Bir Es Suera and took up positions, the area being mainly salt marshes. The El Agheila position was directly in front and facing us about 700 yards away were Italians with a stiffening of Germans. Due to the supply problem, orders were given that ammunition could not be fired unless attacked. After a short while the Italians began to realize this and started to take liberties. One day, before the heat haze occurred, an Italian climbed out of his trench, raised his hand in the Fascist salute and shouted '*Viva Mussolini.*' Turning his back to us, he dropped his pantaloons and squatted to answer the call of nature. We observed with surprised interest. The next day, this fearsome Italian soldier gave a repeat performance. This was going too far for Frank Dollin and he said, '*We're not taking that!*' The following day our range-taker, Chris Shambrook ensured that we had the correct distance, and Frank expertly laid his Vickers on the correct spot. Being good soldiers, we had some spare ammunition. As we waited, a jeep pulled up and out got Brigadier Douglas Graham, the Officer Commanding 153 Brigade. He immediately wanted to know what was going on, so the situation was explained about trying to teach this Italian a lesson and also that we had some spare ammunition. He said, '*All right, but you had better not miss!*' Our Italian did not let us down. He jumped up to what was to be his third performance and although he did not know it, his finale. While he began to exalt his love for *Il Duce*, Frank made final adjustments to the Vickers. Suddenly, the Brigadier's telephone began to sound, but he ignored it! The Italian duly dropped his trousers, Frank fired a short burst and the Italian fell headfirst into his trench. The Brigadier laughed and congratulated us. A wound in the bottom is not generally life threatening, but the next time that Italian used the toilet, he would have to decide which hole to wipe. When the Brigadier returned the call from HQ, they asked why he had not answered. He said, '*I was busy watching my men shoot an I-tie up the arse!*'

Christmas 1942 was spent at the El Agheila position. It was cloudy and cold but there was an open-air Church parade where the CO read the lesson and a new Middlesex Padre, Captain E.C.J. Gibbs, gave the address. The day was declared a holiday and 'C' Company held a swimming gala, but I never volunteered for anything! This was followed by the dinner of roast turkey and pork, Christmas pudding and half-a-pint of beer.

Three days later, 'C' Company went out on an exercise called 'Driver' which was an attack on defences based on those found at Mersa Brega. Two days later this was repeated in another exercise, 'Cleek', the difference being that it was staged at dawn.

On 2 January, Lieutenant General Bernard Montgomery visited the battalion and watched 'C' Company firing on the range. Accompanied by Major General Wimberley, he also watched a 12 Platoon shoot from an Observation Point. Everyone was rewarded with cigarettes.

We sat in this position for about three weeks. The desert far out to our left was considered to be impassable terrain for wheeled vehicles due to the soft sand. However, the word 'impassable' was not in the New Zealander's vocabulary. A Captain Wyler of the unstoppable 2nd New Zealand Division had found and mapped a route through that came out behind the enemy. It became known as 'Wyler's Gap'. When this outflanking movement was carried out, it gave the Axis forces no option but to pull out of the El Agheila position.

On 11 January 'C' Company was again attached to 153 Brigade and we headed off for Wadi Chebir, a Wadi being an Arabic term for a valley, although it can also refer to a dried riverbed. Three days later, 12 Platoon was attached to the 5/7th Gordons. Again, we followed up the Germans and just fired at rearguard actions. Once more, the main problem encountered was anti-personnel and anti-tank mines that were strewn everywhere, and these prevented an immediate chase. They caused a hell of a lot of casualties.

About eighty miles on from El Agheila (and mid-way between Tripoli and the Egyptian frontier) we encountered with amused disbelief, Mussolini's extravaganza, christened 'The Marble Arch' by the British.

The *Afrika Korps* was again in full retreat and Tripoli was now the ultimate prize. Each General wanted to be the first to enter Tripoli and this became a race between the New Zealanders coming in from the flank and the 51st Highland Division. Of course, General Wimberley was determined that the HD would get there first, so it was a case of '*Push on regardless of the consequences. Keep going!*'

As usual, the convoy of trucks churned up an enormous amount of sand and so we were covered from head to foot in dust. What with that and the flies! While the driver did all the driving everyone else had to maintain a good lookout because there were plenty of Axis stragglers about. The Italians of course were not a problem, it was the Germans you had to keep an eye out for. The *Afrika Korps* was rapidly withdrawing along the coast road in commandeered Italian transport, leaving their luckless allies to walk and as we moved up, I saw a typical example of Italian despondency. A column of around a thousand men were walking along and behind them was one Australian soldier. And he had an Italian carrying his rifle! Of course there was nowhere for them to go and no food and water, so they had to march wherever they were told.

The pursuit just went on and on, even though movement was very difficult because of demolitions on the road, and off it due to a heavy rainstorm.

After travelling a distance of around 250 miles from El Agheila, we reached a place called Homs, which was only about thirty-five miles from Tripoli. The main German and Italian positions were around ten miles away, where they had occupied some very high hills to the west of Homs.

On 20 January, supporting the 5th Seaforths in an approach on these hills, an attempt was made to push through a valley at night, but we were ambushed by a very strong German and Italian rearguard. The hillsides were so steep that our Vickers could not be elevated far enough to fire back. The enemy was just dropping their mortars down onto this road, causing very heavy casualties. We were being decimated. The Germans were 'red hot' with a mortar. Whereas artillery fire could be adjusted by about fifty yards, mortars could be adjusted in just yards. One shot might land well away, but then the next one would be a little closer, the next a little closer until the feeling came that the next one was going to fall directly on you. We always thought they could put one in your back pocket if they wanted. They could also be heard distinctly when fired because they made a 'WHOOMP'. The mortar probably caused more casualties than any other weapon.

Lieutenant Wigan turned the platoon around and withdrew about 300 yards back down the road. Everyone had just dismounted to consider what to do, when suddenly a jeep came tearing up to us and stopped. It contained General Wimberley. He was always up towards the front line doing various things, in fact during the advance I had seen him with a shovel, filling in a hole that the Germans had blown in the road. He jumped out and said, 'Who's that?' 'The Middlesex, Sir.' 'Where are you going?' 'We've just been ambushed, so we've turned around to get organized.' Now of all people, he picked on me. 'What's your name Lance Corporal?' so I told him. 'Where do you come from?' 'Finchley, Sir.' 'Do you want to go back to Finchley?' 'Yes, Sir.' He said, 'Well the only way you're going to get *back there is to turn around, go back through those hills, reach Tripoli, then on to Berlin. And then you can go home to Finchley. Do you understand?'* I said, '*Yes, Sir!'* '*So go on then, turn around!'* Wimberley disappeared in a cloud of dust towards the fighting. Not a word had been said to Lieutenant Wigan, who had managed to stay in the shadows.

We reluctantly turned our vehicles around and set off again. After a short distance a track lead off the road to the left. It was just wide enough for a 15cwt truck to go up. We considered this the best way to go, at least until it got light, and proceeded as quietly as possible. We were completely on our own. Initially, the sounds of fighting were in front of us, then to the side and when finally in our rear, it was time to stop. Dawn was about to break. Lieutenant Wigan decided that he and I would climb to the top of the nearest hill to observe. This we began to do, but the slope was so steep that it was impossible to stand up, and thereby forced us to crawl on all fours. Upon reaching the top and looking over the summit, we could not believe our eyes. Laid out in a valley below us was the entire enemy rearguard, mostly Italian, but with German gunners, all their artillery and mortars and about six Italian *Lancia* 10-ton trucks to take away the Italian infantry. Lieutenant Wigan called for the Vickers and ammunition to be hauled to the crest, also sending a runner back to stop the first vehicle that possessed a wireless set to inform HQ of our position and that unless previously attacked we would open fire on the enemy position in one hour. It took a long time and a lot of effort to get the machine guns up the hill with sufficient ammunition, but they were set up and then there was nothing to do but sit, wait and observe. After some time, smoke could be seen coming from a field kitchen and eventually the enemy soldiers began to line up for breakfast. This target could not be allowed to pass. All four machine guns opened fire.

At this stage our CO, Lieutenant Colonel Stephenson, arrived at the bottom of the hill. He wanted to know what was happening. I thought 'Why doesn't he come up here and have a bloody look for himself,' but he did not come up the hill. We had to give him a running commentary

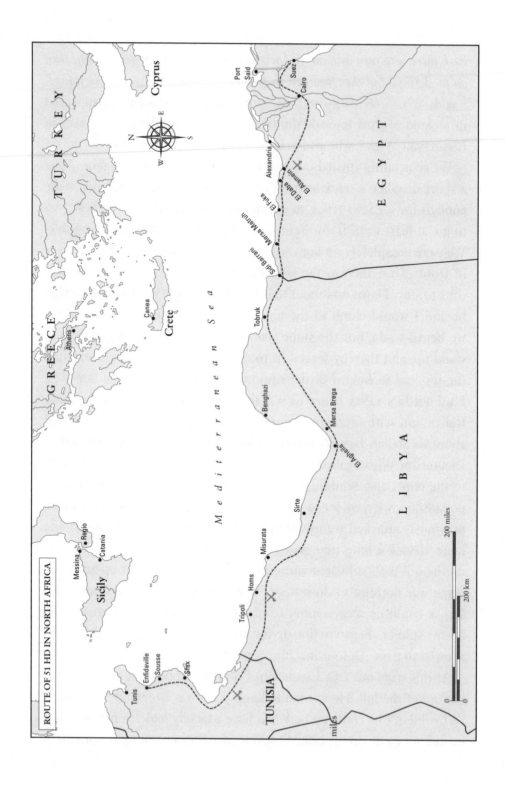

ROUTE OF 51 HD IN NORTH AFRICA

on what was happening. There was a severe loss of life for the trapped enemy. Some of the survivors were trying to pack up and withdraw, but they were in complete disorder. Various figures rushed to board the Lancia trucks, but we had also noticed that the only track exiting this Wadi ran around the side of our hill. Consequently, a Vickers had been lined up on this gap and as the first truck came tearing around, the machine gun opened fire. The truck skidded and turned on its side, blocking the track and preventing all the other vehicles getting out. An Italian Officer subsequently waved a white flag and the firing stopped.[3] This rearguard had had to abandon almost everything.

Meanwhile the 5/7th Gordon Highlanders had advanced and reached us, because the opposition to them had melted away by then. When it was all over, Lieutenant Colonel Stephenson greeted us at the bottom of the hill, telling us how pleased he was, adding '*I must reward you.*' There were about thirty of us in the platoon and he gave us a packet of fags to share between us. '*Have these on me, boys,*' he said. The packet was not even full. These fags, called 'Victory Vs', were made in Egypt and everyone thought they contained camel dung. Even the locals wouldn't smoke them. We actually used camel dung for cooking. It burned very well.

The 5th Black Watch then arrived to round up the prisoners, who amounted to approximately 200 Italians and exactly three Germans. When the captured Italian lorries were inspected, several were found to be loaded with a vast amount of tomato puree. This was another dubious 'reward' because subsequently our cook put this tomato puree, which I hated, in every meal for a bloody month![4]

* * *

---

3. Lieutenant Wigan was awarded the Military Cross for this action.
4. Only recently, I was cooked some spaghetti bolognese by my eldest son, John. I only had a few spoonfuls and started to feel ill. As John said, I looked so bad that he thought the Italians had finally got me!

At 0530 hours on 23 January 1943, the 1st Gordon Highlanders, riding on tanks of the 40th Royal Tank Regiment, entered Tripoli, the New Zealanders following soon after. The 11th Hussars, the 'Cherrypickers', also said that they got into Tripoli first.

Our desert uniform was of course very similar to that worn by the Germans, so as we moved towards the town, the Libyans were very confused. They did not know whether to give us a salute or an outstretched arm. Naturally, as we drove along everyone would give them the Hitler salute and they would all immediately reply in kind!

Unfortunately for us, at this time Lieutenant Wigan was promoted and moved to command another Company.

*   *   *

After this period of fighting, all the troops were billeted in the desert at Ain Zara. Our trenches were dug and canopies put over the top. The platoon was filthy, having not been able to have a wash or change of clothes for six weeks and we were lousy. A new officer arrived, one Captain Herbert, probably from the Nile Delta, who had not seen any fighting and so was spic and span. He took one look at us and said to the sergeant, '*I've never seen such a disgusting crowd in my life. Why are your men not washed and shaved?*' He replied '*Because we haven't got any water.*' He said, '*They get tea don't they? Tell them to drink one half and shave in the other!*' We were only given tea a couple of times a day. We took our shirts off, turned them inside out and watched the sun draw the lice out of the seams. Those men that smoked had the First World War pastime of sticking a cigarette on them because they exploded with a pop!

Three weeks later Captain Herbert did not return from a recce patrol. He was killed when someone trod on an anti-personnel mine. His place was taken by Captain 'Lofty' Pearson, who was to prove what can only be described as one of the finest officers in the British Army. He was brave but also knew how to handle men.

Once 'cleaned up' the 1/7th Middlesex spent about a week in Tripoli, although as we had to work through the night and sleep by day, I did not see anything of it. This time was spent unloading assault landing ships that were coming along the coast with food and petrol because the port had not been badly damaged. The petrol was in containers called 'flimsies' which were metallic, very shiny, and held four gallons. They were so thin that when they were not full, the sides could be pushed in. These 'flimsies' were used once and then thrown away. Of course, they had been knocked about a bit and the seals could not have been 'watertight' as each person could only stay below deck for about an hour because of the fumes. Eventually it was decided that due to so much petrol being lost, the German 'jerrycan' would be copied. In fact, during our journey across the desert we had 'confiscated' any jerrycans left behind because they were better than the two–gallon cans carried on the trucks. A jerrycan carried about four and a half gallons, could be easily carried and was far more robust.

Anyway, most of our time on board these ships was spent trying to find the tinned food, especially peaches. If a box was dropped and they were damaged, it would be a case of '*They can't be issued like that, but we'll take care of them!*'

*   *   *

Towards the end of the month the war 'restarted' and we again moved towards the front, leaving Tripolitania and crossing into Tunisia. The road to the frontier was good, but from that point to Ben Gardane it was nothing more than a cart track. This was the main Army axis road and so was liberally marked with typical Eighth Army signs. One of them read '*Confucious, him say my brother never read signs – my brother bloody fool!*'

Ben Gardane was north of Medenine, a key town on the Mareth Line fortifications erected many years before by the French to keep out the Italians. We took up positions in front of it covering the north and north-west approaches. A few days later, we passed through Ben

Gardane itself as part of a general move forward to make contact with
the enemy. The 7th Armoured Division had bounced the Germans out
of Medenine by moving up quickly, before they really knew what was
happening and they were determined to get it back.

As March arrived, the intelligence information was that Rommel
was going to attack with the 10th Panzer Division. Preparations had
been made for the Middlesex to take up four defensive strongpoints to
cover the anti-tank obstacle of Wadi Zessar. 'B' Company was located
on a feature known as the Abdallah, while 13 and 14 Platoons of 'D'
Company were placed on a commanding position called the Menouble
feature, with 'A' Company covering the southern and south-western
approaches to this. Due to the lack of mines, a dummy minefield was
laid out in front of the position.

There were about four miles between the two opposing forces, so 12
Platoon, together with a platoon of 5/7th Gordons were sent forward
two miles to act as a screen, provide advance warning of the attack and
harass the enemy without getting too involved. If this occurred then it
was to be back on the trucks and through the gaps in the 'minefield' to
our defensive positions behind the wire. 11 Platoon was to cover our
withdrawal.

The night of 2 March was spent 'out in front', behind the only
prominent sand dune, with lookouts posted at the top. The next day,
by mid-morning the heat was becoming unbearable and it was my turn
to be lookout. While I was up there the cook made some porridge, so
Captain Pearson called me down to get some. Having got the porridge
I started to ascend the sand dune with mess tin in hand and at that
moment a rain of enemy smoke shells fell all around, blowing sand
into my porridge. I called out to the Captain to let him know what had
happened and he said, '*Well get yourself some more.*' So I came back
down, got another mess tin of porridge and sat there eating it. I delayed
my return for as long as possible until 'Lofty' said it was about time I
went back up, which I did. When I looked over the crest, to my horror
there were about 300 Italian infantry advancing and they were only

about 500 yards away. I called out something unrepeatable and 'Lofty' came up immediately and had a look for himself. The four guns were mounted in the back of the 15cwt trucks, and so they were driven up the reverse slope and by the time the guns were set up at the top of the dune, they were only 300 yards from us. Completely unsuspecting, they ambled towards us. All four Vickers guns then opened fire for about ten minutes, with devastating results. Lying in the desert were about sixty Italian bodies, the rest of them fled.

The guns were loaded back onto the trucks and together with the Gordons, there was a rapid withdrawal, eventually passing through the gap in our dummy minefield. Waiting at the other end was Brigadier Graham, whom we had met at El Agheila. He stopped us and said, '*Well done. I was watching you and I was watching the Italians advancing. What discipline. 600 yards, you held your fire. 500 yards, still held your fire. I thought 'What fire discipline these Middlesex have got'. 400 yards and I thought 'They must open fire now'. No, you waited until they were 300 yards away and then let them have it. Well done. I wish I had a few more like you.*'

We thought it best not to mention that the enemy had not been seen because I was eating porridge.

The next few days were spent performing similar 'carrier screen' operations plus harassing shoots, but on 6 March, tanks of the 10th Panzer Division, carrying out its first attack in Tunisia, drove towards us. On reaching the dummy minefield they hesitated, decided not to take the chance and turned to their left, moving along the side of the wire to try to find a gap, thereby presenting the sides of their vehicles to an area defended by the 101 Guards Brigade. The anti-tank guns destroyed fifty-two of them before the panzers admitted defeat and withdrew.

Ten days later our own attacks commenced and by 20 March the drive for Tunis was truly under way.

We moved forward along the coast for about twenty-five miles to Gabes. Just beyond it was a twenty-mile area between the sea and some salt marshes, known as the Gabes Gap, which was heavily defended by the Germans and Italians. However, once again the New Zealand

Division made a left hook inland, outflanking these defences and causing the enemy to withdraw behind another Wadi, the Wadi Akarit. This dropped down about fifteen feet, stretched across half-a-mile and then went up fifteen feet. Beyond it were the Mat-Marta Hills, where the Axis forces were positioned, although the Germans put the Italians in front. As usual, they were dispensable.

The move began on 6 April, with the 4th Indian Division performing the main attack. Although my Brigade was just holding the line, it was our task to move up close to the Wadi and engage known enemy strongpoints while the Gurkhas of the Indian Division went through on a night attack. Of course they got right amongst these Italians and their screams and shouts could be heard right back across the Wadi.

The enemy counter fire was heavy and there were a lot of artillery and mortar shells landing around us, and we all kept down when the Vickers were not required to fire. My friend Johnny Hunt, the one who had accidentally shot me during the final withdrawal to the Dunkirk beach, was in the two-man trench beside mine, about six feet away. Even after all this time, he was continually saying, '*I didn't mean to shoot you, Jeff!*' no matter how much I assured him that I knew he hadn't.

The following morning, I stood up but Johnny did not. I looked into his hole. Either a shell or a mortar bomb had exploded right on the edge. There was nothing left of him, not even a sign of his identity discs. Of course, it was hot and did not take long for the flies and other things to arrive. With nothing to dig out, there was no point in digging another hole for a grave, so I said to everyone, '*We'll just have to fill it in and mark it. The registration people will come along after the battle and find it.*' All we had to mark the spot was a piece of wood from a ration box.[5, 6]

---

5. It was not until many years after the war, when I found a book that gave all the Middlesex casualties and their cemeteries that I realized he was on the list of No Known Graves in the War Cemetery at Medjez-el-Bab. Sadly, the marker must have been blown away or something. I know he had a wife and little girl. He was 29 years old.

6. The ferocity of the fighting around us can be judged by the award of the Victoria Cross to Lieutenant Colonel Lorne-Campbell of the Argyll and Sutherland Highlanders,

During that morning we watched as the Gurkhas continued to chase the Italians around the hills. After this we only had to tell the Italians that the Gurkhas were going to attack and they packed up even quicker than before.

Then there was another move forward. Once more, the New Zealanders attacked around to the rear towards a place called El Hamma. The Germans and Italians were more or less cut off and so had to withdraw as fast as they could, but their problem was the lack of roads. Off the road was soft sand, and they had to pass rapidly through El Hamma itself.

Eventually we pushed fifty miles up the coast to Sfax and another eighty miles to Sousse, only to find them already occupied by the New Zealanders.

Then it was twenty-five miles on to the mountains of Enfidaville, where both sides half-heartedly fired a few shots, so that honour was satisfied. However, on 29 April one of my blokes, thirty-one-year-old Corporal Bill King, an old man to us, was killed by fragments from a mortar bomb.[7]

* * *

The Highland Division relieved the 4th Indian Division, and in our case the Rashapatutna Rifles. In this position we had to go back at night to pick up our rations for the next day and return with them in daylight. On the first trip we saw an old Arab hut that had loads of chickens running around, so naturally our thoughts were 'We'll have them!' If any of us had had the sense, we would have stopped to think 'Why are these chickens being allowed to run around when there are all these troops about?' However, everyone went in and started grabbing the chickens, only to realize that the place was absolutely full of fleas. Everybody immediately lost interest in the chickens and ended up running naked around the mountain trying to get rid of the fleas!

---

the only such decoration to the Highland Division during the entire war.
7. Bill King is buried in the Enfidaville War Cemetery, Grave IV.A.31.

Shortly after, with Bizerta and Tunis having fallen to the First Army, we heard that the Germans in North Africa had capitulated. I could not believe it. I had survived, but almost immediately the thought came, 'Why me?'

* * *

Corporal Tommy Roberts was the driver for Lieutenant Colonel Stephenson. Somewhere along the journey from Alamein, the Colonel had acquired an Italian motorhome, but had not been able to bring it forward all the way to where we had advanced. With the fighting over, he decided to have this vehicle brought up. He sent Tommy for it, along with a chap called Oliver Bliss. There had to be two of them of course, one to drive the vehicle they travelled in and the other to bring the motorhome back. If there was anyone in the battalion who knew how to bend rules and the King's Regulations it was Ollie. The motorhome had been left quite a way back and so it meant being away for a couple of nights. On the way there, they had to stay in a transit camp and when it came to being fed, found that the food was absolutely terrible. The next day they picked up the motorhome and while inspecting the interior, discovered that the Colonel had left a couple of valises in it. Ollie opened them and told Tommy, *'We're not going to eat corned beef stew on the way back.'* When they reached the transit camp they put on two of the Colonel's uniforms, walked into the Officer's Mess and had a slap-up meal! Unfortunately, upon leaving, two Red Caps were waiting and arrested them for impersonating officers. This was reported to Colonel Stephenson, who persuaded the Red Caps to let him deal with the two imposters. When they arrived back at the battalion, the Colonel said, *'What have you got to say for yourselves?'* They said, *'We wanted a decent meal, so we borrowed your uniforms.'* Stephenson said, *'Now that's what I call initiative and that's what I want in my battalion, men with initiative. Get out of here and don't do it again!'*

Stephenson was quite a character and a famous pre-war cricketer who bowled for Essex. He always carried a cricket ball in his pocket and prior to one particular attack, during an Orders Group, where everyone was informed about what was going to happen, he said '*Don't worry. If we run out of ammunition, I'll throw my balls at them. I never miss!*' It broke the tension. After that, at any further Orders Groups he would say, '*Are there any questions?*' and there would always be someone who asked '*Colonel, have you got your balls with you?*' And he'd reply, '*Yes. And I never miss!*'[8]

*   *   *

After a short time we moved into Algeria and headed for Djidjelli on the Atlantic coast for training on landing craft. The weather was lovely, so we never took things too seriously and spent a lot of time swimming in the sea.

---

8. Years later I read a newspaper article where someone was ridiculing him over the cricket ball. They took it seriously. It was ONLY a gimmick!

Chapter Seven

Sicily

On 4 July we moved to a transit camp at Sousse in preparation for our next operation, which of course was a secret. Everyone was provided with translation books for Greek. The next day we marched eight miles to the Sousse docks, where the native workers informed us, '*You're not going to Greece, you're going to Sicily!*'

Standing with all my equipment and slowly melting in the African sun, Colonel Stephenson, who was not initially coming with us, stopped in front of me and said, '*Lance Corporal, can you tell me how many razor blades you've got?*' Not believing my ears, I asked him to repeat what he had said. He repeated '*How many razor blades have you got?*' Not knowing, but being a good soldier, I told a lie. '*Four, Sir.*' '*Will you be able to shave every day?*' '*Oh yes, Sir.*' '*Good show,*' he said, '*we don't want to appear unshaven in front of the I-ties do we?*' He then moved down the line to look for his next victim. I'm sure that helped us in the occupation of Sicily.

After embarking on LCIs, Landing Craft Infantry, we set sail at 1300 hours. The journey was on a very calm sea and the convoy duly arrived in Malta during the late afternoon of the next day. The Company moved to a transit camp that was four miles from Valetta where each man was immediately issued with fifty cigarettes and three bottles of beer! Everyone had some free time for a visit to Valetta, which had been bombed to bits, but neither I, nor Frank Dollin had any money, so we couldn't do much.

On 9 July we moved back to Valetta harbour, re-embarked and set sail for Sicily at 0830 hours. This time the sea was incredibly rough. We did everything except loop the loop. The LCIs were like tin boxes and the waves crashed against them, causing them to roll all over the place. Everybody was sick except me, and I was having a good laugh at them. I began to eat my dinner when all of a sudden I vomited straight into my mess tin! I felt absolutely terrible and of course received plenty of joyous stick from the others.

The following morning at 0600 hours, the Brigade started landing at Pachino on the Cape Passero, at the south-eastern tip of the island. The LCIs came in pretty close to the shore, the front ramp was lowered and I jumped into the water. It came up to about my knees and I walked towards the shore, where everyone was waddling around like ducks because our trousers were full of water and the gaiters helped keep it in. I stood on a rock and heaved my heart up. Looking round, blokes everywhere were being sick. If there had been a troop of Girl Guides there, they would have pushed us back into the sea, but fortunately it was only the Italians.

A very nice journalist chap called Alan Whicker came with us towards our first objective which was a place called Noto, about fifteen miles up the coast. The route forward went up in terraces, passing through vineyards of unripe grapes and after being in the desert, it seemed like paradise to us. No one had seen any fruit for ages, so as we moved up the terraces, everyone was grasping handfuls of grapes and eating them greedily.

Within a mile of the beach, we approached a village and took up position. I was now the Number 1 on the gun. Through the hills about 500 yards away, we could see a church steeple with a bell in it. There was a only little a bit of firing going on, so Frank Dollin, the Number 1 on the other gun, said, '*Do you reckon you could hit that bell with a Vickers? A single shot.*' So we had a bet on who could hit it first. He fired one round and missed. I fired a round from my gun and missed. He then fired a burst and hit this bell, which of course consequently went 'Ding, dong, ding, dong.' This must have been the signal for the I-ties to evacuate the place, because they all began jumping out of their trenches and streaming away!

Three hours further on, the fruit took effect. The resulting view was one of dropped trousers and white arses poking out of vines as its impact on our empty stomachs caused diarrhoea. It was again fortunate that there were no Germans in the area.

Noto was the first large village encountered after the landing and was virtually undamaged. The locals were bewildered by our arrival. In an instant they changed from being supporters of Mussolini to members of Churchill's fan club.

Advancing through Palazzolo and Vizzini, we reached the Catania Plain. There we met the Herman Goring Parachute Division, which had been flown in from southern France and our days of eating grapes were over. They contested every yard. The heat was intense and many scrubland fires were started by the exploding shells and mortar bombs.

The German Airfield at Gerbini on the inland slopes of Mount Etna was reached, and during the night of 20 - 21 July, an attack went in. The platoon was following the Seaforth Highlanders to consolidate the position, but it was impossible for them to clear every trench in darkness and as I jumped over a two-man slit trench, a bloody German lying in it shot me up the arse with a Luger. I fell down, but it did not hurt at first, just stung. Following behind was our First-Aid bloke, a little Jewish boy called Nobby Novitt. I had khaki drill uniform on, so he pulled my shorts down and I said, '*Is it all there Nobby?*' He said, '*Yeah, but I don't think you'll be using it for a while!*' He then said, '*How am I going to bandage that up?*' I said, '*You'll have to hang it over my shoulder!*' I was carried on a stretcher to an ambulance and driven away to a Dressing Station. That was the end of my Sicilian campaign.

I was immediately transported to an airstrip at Catania and shoved into the back of a Dakota full of wounded. The airfield was grass and when the plane took off, it was going at about 100 miles an hour and the grass was passing by my head. All the blood rushed from my feet to my head! A First-Aid bloke beside me kept on saying, '*I hope we don't bump into any German fighters. There are no guns on this plane.*' I said,

'*Well it's got a Red Cross on it.*' He said, '*They don't take any notice of that!*'

When the plane came in to land at Tunis he carried on. '*Look at all those wrecked aircraft, crashed while trying to land.*' Just the sort of bloke you need to cheer you up on a flight like that.

Everyone was put on an Arab hospital train adorned with big Red Crosses. This proceeded to move for a few hundred yards and then stop for three hours. The Arab train driver would get out, make tea from the boiling water, then pray to Allah before deciding to move on a little bit further. During the journey some Arabs tried to raid the train to see what they could steal. As there were no armed guards on board, when the Arabs got close, the men that were capable threw anything they could at them, including tins of bully beef. Lying down, I was unable to help them. Some of these Arabs would steal anything. Sometimes, after the fighting had finished, they would dig up the dead bodies and take the uniforms off them. The bodies would be left on the ground and whatever desert creatures were about would eat them.

After five days on this train, it arrived in Constantine, Algeria, and I was taken to an old French hospital, now run by the British. It was here that a 9mm bullet was removed.

The hospital had an English matron, a great big woman who was worse than any sergeant major I had ever known. I think the idea was that everyone was to become so frightened of her, they just wanted to get back to the front line where it was safer.

When people were well enough, they were let out into the local town. Another of my blokes, Ginger Richardson, was also in the hospital. He was a native of Newcastle and had been posted to us from the Royal Northumberland Fusiliers. Half the time I could not understand a word he said. He had been at the siege of Tobruk and was a bit 'bomb happy'. While we were walking around the town, an American deserter came up to us and said, '*Are you boys looking for anything?*' '*It depends what you've got.*' '*Do you want booze?*' because of course being a Muslim country, they did not drink alcohol. He showed us to an

Arab flat, took some money and came back with a bottle. I have no idea what it contained, probably anti-freeze. We drank it and he asked if we wanted any more. He took some more money off us. After tasting the second bottle Ginger said, '*We're not paying for this rot-gut. Give us our money back.*' There were also a couple of Arabs in the room and they started shouting, so Ginger pulled out an Italian Beretta revolver that he had acquired and fired a shot through the ceiling. He said, '*The next one's going through your bloody head! Give us our money back.*' He got his money back all right and the Arabs left rather quickly!

After a few weeks, thankfully it was discharge time and the two of us were transferred to a transit camp in the First Army area. They were still into blancoing white stones, asking permission to speak to an officer and all that kind of rubbish. There was an NCO who had never seen action, who looked at us and said, '*Experienced NCOs. Just what I need to run this camp.*' We thought '*Not us!*' Consequently, we tried to continually do things wrong so that he would get rid of us. The camp was full of soldiers straight out from England, and what succeeded for us involved the beer ration. As each person only got one bottle of beer a week, we would say to these rookies, '*Do you want to go on guard tonight?*' Of course, they would say '*No corporal.*' So we said, '*Well give us your bottle of beer then.*' We took their beer off them and made sure they did not get any fatigues. One of them reported us to this officer, who said, '*It was disgusting,*' and started lecturing us, saying, '*It was no way to act. You Eighth Army soldiers are scruffy and have no discipline or respect.*' I answered, '*No, but we know how to fight. We've come 2,000 miles from Alamein to get here. How far has your mob come? If you don't like us, get rid of us! We don't like it here and the only thing we want to do is get out of it.*' He just walked away in disgust.

* * *

The 51st Highland Division was one of three veteran Divisions that Montgomery wanted to employ for the invasion of Europe and so they had been transported back to England. Under Monty's orders, all

My mother is on the left. Pictured with her mother and sister.

Shortly after joining the 1/7th Middlesex.

Sporting the HD Patch in 1941. Myself, Ken Davies and Reg Lyons.

Holland 1945. Harry Alcock, Tommy Tubbs, Roy Holmwood, Dennis Daly and Myself.

Myself, Christopher Coyne, the cook, a reinforcement, Tommy Tubbs, 'Whispering Grass' (he had a very hoarse voice!). Front row: Dennis Daly, The Duke and Harry Alcock.

A typical Middlesex Regiment Vickers in action, Holland 1944. We always wore our berets.

Waiting to cross the Rhine. Chris Coyne and Roy Holmwood. Note the smoke screen in the background.

Being presented with the MM ribbon by Montgomery. Taken by a friend in the audience (the official photographer was changing his film!).

B. L. Montgomery
Field-Marshal

Standing just behind and to the right of Monty, amongst all those presented with awards at the ceremony.

Germany 1945, with Sgt Fred Addison MM.

Must have been bored. Putting ammunition back into the belts.

Portrait, 1945.

Meeting Monty again. Colleville–Montgomery, 1997.

Middlesex group outside the Café Gondree. Dennis Daly, Arthur Berry (RA), Arlette Gondree, myself, Major Alan Carter and Bill Jones.

The Middlesex
Regiment Memorial
in Cuverville.

The former graves of
Luxton and Philbin.
Alan Carter talks to the
owner, Andre Cenedese,
who maintained this
shrine even after the
men had been moved to
Ranville Cemetery.

At the presentation
of a Vickers machine
gun to the village of
Cuverville. Myself,
Major Alan Carter,
Dennis Daly and Bill
Jones.

The Vickers presented.

Post war – on the buses.

Laying a wreath on the 51st Highland Division Memorial, opposite the notorious Chateau St Come.

At the Le Mesnil Brickworks, 2009.

Standing below St. Joseph's church tower in Kartsheuvelle. The repaired brickwork can still be seen where two tank shells entered and departed, one of them just missing my legs.

With Ivy on our Wedding Day, 25th September 1948.

With our sons, John and Keith in Bruges.

members left behind were also to be returned to their own units, so all the 'odd and sods' such as us were collected and sent to Algiers to wait for a ship to take everyone home. Arriving in Algiers, we went to a big, tented camp on the racecourse. When a sufficient number was raised [a draft] we embarked on a boat called the *Monarch of Bermuda*. On board were a few other Middlesex men, so we linked up.

While waiting to leave, one of the crew said to us, '*See that ship there, it's called* the Duchess of Bedford. *It's jinxed! There's always things happening to it.*' That night the convoy set sail.

The following morning we saw that the *Duchess of Bedford* was alongside us. A little later, our Middlesex group had had lunch and we were walking along the long promenade deck when the ship suddenly appeared to alter course, which was not unusual as convoys had to zigzag to avoid U-Boats. Then we noticed the *Duchess of Bedford* coming towards us. I said to the others, '*If it doesn't change direction soon, it's going to hit us,*' and then it became obvious that it *was* going to hit us. We immediately tore back along the deck to try and get on the other side of the ship. The deck seemed like it was ten miles long, and just as we got to the top, it struck us, smashing all the lifeboats that were hanging over the side. We could hear the side of the ship coming in. There were a lot of French civilians on board travelling to England and what a panic. The crew themselves got in the remaining lifeboats. If it was not for the Army, the boat would have sunk! They were the only ones who did what they were told. Luckily, it was a glancing blow and so not enough damage was done to sink us. Apparently the steering of the *Duchess of Bedford* had gone wrong. Eventually, they sent us all below and looking out of a porthole the jinxed ship could be seen getting further away, thank goodness. However, it was *us* leaving the convoy, being left behind with the damage. A destroyer towed the ship into Gibraltar and we stayed there for three or four days while they made temporary repairs.

Just across the bay was the Spanish town of Algeciras and of course they were friendly towards Hitler, so to avoid letting them find out that the ship was full of troops, we were not allowed on deck. Everyone was really fed up having to stay below deck all day, although they did let us out a little at night. After the repairs (I think they filled the hole with concrete), the ship went on a trial run around Gibraltar Harbour and got a big rope tangled around a propeller and so had to return immediately. We wondered if the ship would ever get back to England. Then one night, all of sudden the engines started up and the ship made a mighty leap forward and away we went. The ship was alone, but we were informed that it was too fast for a U-Boat to catch it.

And so, after a mad dash across the ocean, on Christmas Eve 1943 the *Monarch of Bermuda* docked in Greenock, the place where I had set out, so ending my days as a Desert Rat.

*   *   *

The North African campaign had cost the 1/7th Middlesex Regiment 263 casualties, 100 of which had been killed. Overall, the 51st Highland Division suffered 5,339 casualties, including 1,071 killed.

In Sicily, the 1/7th Middlesex had 60 casualties, with 12 of those killed. The HD had 1312 casualties, including 124 killed.

Chapter Eight

D-Day and Normandy

The following day I proceeded on fourteen days disembarkation leave, which I spent at my sister Joan's house in Barnet. I also went to see my mother a few times at Woodford Green. The sister of the door-to-door salesman had had a greengrocer's shop in Woodford Green, and I can only assume that she died because he ended up with it. This chap and my mother now lived together at the shop. She worked in it, while he had changed jobs and was now a postman, quite a good job.

I then received orders to report to Two Waters at Hemel Hempstead where the 1/7th Middlesex had been billeted. It was an empty housing estate filled with troops. 'Lofty' Pearson, now a Major, had taken over command of 'C' Company. My old comrades knew that I was rejoining them and so Frank Dollin had organized a tour of the local pubs as a celebration. After having my fair share of beer I returned to the billet, an empty house we had been given and went upstairs to bed. During the night I needed to answer the call of nature and not being used to sleeping in a house for so long, saw a patch of light which I took to be the door and stepped through it. This 'door' was an upstairs window and I landed in the garden below. A guard who was patrolling the estate found me in the roses! If I had been sober I would probably have killed myself, but the only damage done was to my ego.

Hemel Hempstead proved to be a delightful town. At first the inhabitants were apprehensive about our arrival. They thought that troops coming back from the desert who knew they were going to be involved in the Second Front, would be getting drunk and causing all sorts of problems, but it was just the opposite. In fact, I actually had a girlfriend there. My mates had fixed her up for me before I arrived back! She was Jewish, a nice girl called Lucy Goldberg, who would come out drinking with us. One day she said, '*You will have to come home, meet my parents and have a meal. It's better than Army food.*' So I was taken home a few times. During one of these visits her father said, '*Don't get too close to my Lucy, because you're not one of us. We would never let her marry you.*' I thought 'arseholes to you,' but they were nice people anyway. Another day when I was there, a relative of theirs who was in the American Army paid a visit. He was a big chap who was absolutely full of what he was and was not going to do to the Germans. Eventually, as we were sitting at the table having dinner, it became too much for Lucy's father and he said, '*For goodness sake shut your big mouth up and listen to this boy here. He's done it.*' The Yank apologized and kept quiet after that.

The subsequent training for the invasion was not taken too seriously. We thought we knew it all. Had we not just beaten the *Afrika Korps*? We knew that we were taking part in the invasion and so wanted to enjoy our time in England. Also, after Sicily, the Highland Division had lost General Wimberley. Due to his knowledge and experience in successfully handling Divisions in wartime conditions, he was appointed to be Commandant of the Staff College at Camberley. Everybody liked 'Big Tam' and his way of doing things. Although he was a bit of a Tartar, you could talk to him. He was a soldier's General and was always where the fighting was heaviest. His replacement was a Lowlander called General David Bullen-Smith. This was not a popular decision within the Division because naturally, the Highlanders did not like the Lowlanders and this went back to when the Jocks were fighting us and the Lowlanders sided with the English. Straight away Bullen-Smith began altering things and of course the Jocks did not like it, especially when he stopped the performance of any Highland dancing! Consequently, Bullen-Smith had got off to a very bad start.

There was the added feeling amongst the three Divisions that Montgomery brought back, the 50th Tyne and Tees Infantry, the 51st

Highland and 7th Armoured that we had done our bit. *'There are all these other Divisions that have been sitting on their arse in England for four years. Let them have a go!'* However, he needed experienced Divisions. Unfortunately, everyone was tired. This was obviously not his fault, but if you are tired before you start, by the time you get to where you are going, you're exhausted.

*   *   *

Our transport, the 15cwt trucks, had been left out in the desert and so we were completely re-equipped, but this time with Bren gun carriers. It was realized in the desert that the platoons needed to be more mobile and also the carriers were thought to be more suitable for use in the mud of North-West Europe. Unfortunately, this was the most uncomfortable vehicle ever invented. It weighed four tons and was track-driven. Although armoured, it was completely open, so the occupants froze in the winter and baked during the summer. A platoon required four carriers to transport the guns and there was also the Platoon Commander's carrier, which also transported the range-taker and runner, plus there was another carrier for the Platoon Sergeant, who continued to bring up the rear. To drive these carriers there had to be what was called a driver-mechanic, in order that he could perform basic maintenance on the vehicle. There was not enough time to train our existing drivers as mechanics, so they were all incorporated into the gun crews to make up the numbers, as they had at least been given basic training on the Vickers. To fill the void an intake of trained drivers was received from the Royal Signals Regiment. One of them, Dennis Daly (who would later become my driver) was rather shocked when he arrived. Coming from Manchester he had never heard of Middlesex. In the Signals, he had come from an environment where they had had to have their trousers creased, stand to attention, step back and disappear type of thing, and all the officers had to be called 'Sir' and the NCOs, 'sergeant' or 'corporal'. He arrived at Hemel Hempstead on a Saturday afternoon and after finding the depot, knocked on the

Company Office door and went in. A corporal was sitting there with his feet up on the table, smoking a fag. He said, '*Hello mate. What do you want?*' '*14320233 Private Daly, reporting for duty.*' The corporal said, '*Well for Christ's sake sit down and don't call me corporal! Where have you come from?*' He told him. '*Have you had anything to eat? No? Well come over to the cookhouse and I'll get the cook to rustle you up a bit of grub.*' So he took him over there and the cook said, '*Dinner's gone, I haven't got much for you,*' and proceeded to cook him egg, bacon, chips, sausages, beans, the lot. There was a hardly a soul about in the depot, so Dennis asked where everyone was. The corporal replied, '*A bloke called Bertie Gee is getting married and they've all gone to London for the wedding.*' Dennis said, '*What, all of them?*' '*Yeah. Major Pearson gave them all a pass because he said, 'They are going to go whether I give them a pass or not, so I'll keep them out of trouble!*' Of course Dennis' immediate thought was 'What sort of unit is this?'

* * *

With the consequent change to carriers, part of our training was 'Carrier Drill'. This included such things as how to get on board, the sequence it was to be carried out in, and how to get off it. You were supposed to get the machine guns off first, then the ammunition. There was a rule for everything! Of course nobody took any notice. We just got on and off how and when.

In the centre of the carrier, on the engine cover was a special mounting with two fixtures for the Vickers and this was how it was transported. It was possible to fire it from the carrier.

All the carriers carried the identification number 64. This was true of all machine-gun battalions no matter the Division to which they were attached.

The 1/7th Middlesex also had a new commanding officer. Colonel Stephenson had been promoted and the battalion was taken over by a little, bandy-legged Regular called Lieutenant Colonel Andrew Man. Like Wimberley, Stephenson had been with us for a long time and everyone had got used to his ways. And so, when this new Colonel arrived with his different methods, it did not go down very well, especially as he started by shouting at people, being a bit 'regimental', standing to attention when talking to him and suchlike. Consequently, he was not particularly liked by the men.

Also, due to lessons learned in the desert, there was a change in the command structure of our platoons. There had been a number of incidents where an infantry Lieutenant had been slightly senior to the machine-gun Lieutenant and had ordered him to site the machine guns in a position that had proved to be an error. Therefore, to prevent the infantry, no matter how well intended, ordering the MG Platoon Officer to put us in a position that might not be the most advantageous for a machine gun, the rank was raised to Captain. Our new officer was a Captain Gibbs.

One good bit of news was that Alan Carter rejoined us. He had contacted the Colonel and said that although he was not in A1 condition, he wanted to come back to the battalion. His stomach wound was certainly not properly healed.

* * *

In late May 1944 amidst many fond farewells from the local females, including Lucy, we left Hemel Hempstead for a concentration area that turned out to be at Wanstead Flats near Whipps Cross. I couldn't believe it, as my mother's place was only a couple of miles away. Unfortunately, there was not supposed to be any contact with the outside world and so we were completely sealed in, the whole site being surrounded by barbed wire and patrolled by the Military Police. However, many of the boys were itching to go home for one last time. Consequently, it was arranged so that some troops would start a fight or a disturbance at one end of the camp and when the MPs rushed towards it, the lads were over the wire at the other end! The buses outside ran right past my mother's house and so it was only a few minutes away. I got home two or three times. Getting back in was a little more difficult, but the wire was not staked that solidly to the ground and providing you were careful, it was possible to get underneath and navigate through the rolls of wire. Of course, sentries were walking around, but there were always blokes who would help you get in and out by holding up the wire.

On 4 June, having had something to eat with Alfie Littlewort, who had been in my platoon for the whole of the desert campaign, we were walking back to our bell tents when he said, '*I don't feel very well. I feel hot and giddy.*' The First-Aid tent was close by so I told him to go in there and get a pill. I stood outside and waited. And waited. Suddenly they brought a bloke out on a stretcher and it was Alf! He suffered from malaria, but in all that time in the desert it had never flared up, yet it had started up now, completely out of the blue.

The following day we boarded 3-Ton lorries that took us to Tilbury Docks to embark for the invasion. The carriers, which had not been with us in the camp, went on a different ship. The reasoning behind this was that if the ship with the carriers was sunk, the machine gunners would still be available, and if the ship carrying the machine gunners was lost, at least they would have the carriers. Quite a comforting thought! The idea was that we would meet up within an hour of landing in Normandy, but knowing the Army as we did after all these years, we all thought 'Some chance of that.'

The journey across was in darkness and again on board a Landing Craft Infantry. It was only here that we received our briefing about the operation. They had probably thought that it was a bit risky to do it in the transit camp with people getting out all the time. We were informed that our destination was Normandy, specifically a beach codenamed *Sword,* near Ouistreham to be precise.

The following day, 6 June, the sea was really rough. We eventually approached *Sword Beach* and were scheduled to land early in the afternoon, but to our dismay the small group of ships to which we belonged turned back three or four miles out and started circling. There was insufficient room for us to land on *Sword,* so the night was spent cruising around off the coast with the German heavy guns at Le Havre amusing themselves by lobbing shells at us.

The next day at about 1700 hours, it was decided that we would land through the Canadians, on *Juno Beach*. It was still rough so the LCI went in closer to the beach, where there was still considerable firing going on. The Canadians had advanced inland about eight miles. Everybody wanted to get to the shore, because it was safer than being stuck on the boat. The assault landing craft came alongside and we stood ready to climb down the scrambling nets. There was a swell of about eight feet and I was amongst the first in the queue to get down the nets. Every time I went to step in the boat I either went down eight feet or the swell came up eight feet. There were enemy shells flying about and the chap above, fed up with my dallying, put a boot on my shoulder and gave me a shove to help me on my way shouting, '*For Christ's sake get on that bloody boat! Let's get off this tub!*' Anyway, I fell in the bottom of the boat. The others got on board and we set off, initially circling round and round. The big guns at Le Havre continued sending over shells, some of which we thought appeared to be aimed directly at us.

The assault craft went in and reached the shore, and although landing on *Juno*, it was right on the border with *Sword Beach*. The ramp went down and out we went into knee-high water. There was no time to think. We just wanted to get off that beach and into some shelter. Everything seemed organized as we ran across the sand, guided by the Naval Beachmasters. We took shelter in the nearest houses along the esplanade. There was no close-quarter fighting in the immediate area, but still plenty of shells landing from the German artillery, and one or two mortar bombs and sniper bullets flying about. Knocked out tanks and vehicles were strewn about the beach. From there we headed inland to our designated meeting point, a road. Our new Platoon Officer, Captain Gibbs, was yet to prove himself to us. His appearance had not exactly engendered confidence in the men up to now and we thought he might be a bit of a 'chinless wonder'. I had told the group to keep their eye on me. However, using his map he quickly and efficiently worked out the route to our rendezvous point.

After staggering and crawling along, we reached a sunken road where Gibbs told us to scrape out some protection in the ground and wait for the carriers, which *nobody* expected to appear. After about an hour, to our amazement a dispatch rider rode up leading our carriers. How on earth they managed it I do not know, especially as the rider was one of the replacements following our losses in the desert, a mad Pole called Fred (Schilowski) who was a bit deaf and did not speak very good English! He shouted something to us in half-English, half-Polish and shot off in a cloud of dust. He wasn't going to hang about. We piled into the carriers and 'C' Company, led by Major Pearson, headed to Banville, about two miles inland. It was dark by the time we were able to dig in for the night.

Orders were then received for the Highland Division to move over to the River Orne area, but in our path was a radar station on a high piece of ground at Douvres-la-Deliverande. Therefore, on the way could we just stop off and capture it! Minefields surrounded the site, so in order to get inland as far and as quickly as possible, the infantry on the initial landing had bypassed it. The site was not supposed to be any real trouble because it was '…*only manned by Luftwaffe personnel. When Germany's Brylcream Boys see you coming, they will probably run away!*' Unfortunately, no one had told the Germans about this. Obviously the Division possessed our machine guns but it did not have 'flail' tanks or specialist armoured vehicles such as bulldozers. We were also informed that none of our own troops were in that specific area. Therefore as we approached the site and soldiers were spotted in camouflaged smocks amongst a group of trees, we opened fire. They fired a few back. As we got a bit closer, I could hear them swearing away in English. I said, '*I know some of the Germans can speak English, but they can't swear like that, surely!*' And so, after having them tell us that our parents were not married, things were sorted out while the Germans looked on with interest at us trying to kill each another. These men turned out to be Canadian Parachutists who had been dropped miles from their Dropping Zone on the other side of the River Orne.

Subsequently, the attack on the site went in and we provided support fire, but those involved suffered over 100 casualties and the Jocks never got near the radar station. The occupants were not just *Luftwaffe*, they had a grenadier battalion dug in there who knew what they were doing! The site had its own 230-man garrison to occupy machine-gun nests, mortar positions, an anti-aircraft battery and a fortified multi-storey subterranean command bunker.

That evening we were suddenly ordered to leave it alone and move to the area of the 6th Airborne Division, east of the River Orne, where our presence was urgently required. Someone else would have to deal with the radar station.[1] And so we moved into Colleville for the night.

Shortly after dawn on 9 June the platoon moved off to Ranville, the first town to be liberated by the Paras. We got there at about 0800 hours and found parachutists wandering about the place. Parking the carriers on the edge of a small wood we began to unload all the kit and guns. One of our drivers, Private Pretty, was helping out when a German officer stepped out of the wood, shot him and stepped back in. Pretty said, '*Here, that bugger's shot me!*' He had been hit in the upper body, but it was not too serious. Some parachutists then went through the wood and cleared the Germans out.

Before there was time to dig our machine guns in, orders arrived to move off immediately and go back to the canal bridge. Positions were taken up along the western bank of the canal, just north of the bridge. As in the desert with the trucks, the carriers pulled back to the rear. We were to give overhead supporting fire to the Paras dug in on the opposite side of the Orne. In effect this was a second-line position, but you did not wander around because there was plenty of stuff still flying about. Some Commandos who were close to us kept saying '*Get

---

1. The radar station resisted all attacks until finally surrendering on 17 June.

down. Keep down.' Typically, Frank Dollin got out to walk somewhere and a Commando officer said to him, '*We don't want to walk about, do we?*' Frank replied, '*If the Germans see us creep about, they might think we're frightened. They'll take liberties!*' The Commando said, '*You can get yourself killed, but not my blokes.*'

That night the *Luftwaffe* amused itself by coming over and dropping what were called Butterfly bombs, anti-personnel devices that had little propellers. As they rotated it sounded like butterflies fluttering down, but unless they landed directly in your trench they could not injure anyone. All our slit trenches were covered over, mostly with corrugated iron. However, 12 Platoon did suffer two casualties from these Butterfly bombs when they were out of their trenches.

On the night of 10 June, 12 Platoon re-crossed the bridges over the canal and the River Orne, this being 300 yards further on, and advanced towards Escoville with the 5/7th Gordons. We took up a position close to the Bois de Bavent, south of a vital road junction called The Triangle.[2] This was an absolutely vital location because it was the road junction between the roads from Troarn to Escoville and Breville, the two main roads from the south-east by which access to the bridges was possible. The 8th Parachute Battalion was in position in the Bois de Bavent itself. The nearest village to us was Herouvillette, which was only 500 yards to the south. To the west was a vast open plain called the *Butte de la Hogue* that had been the designated Dropping Zone for the 8th Parachute Battalion on D-Day. Our arc of fire also covered the villages of Sannerville and Banneville, which were just to the south of Touffreville. All the Vickers work performed previously in the desert was long-range firing, but suddenly here was a totally different scenario, with it all being comparatively short-range firing. This was a certainly a bit of a shock.

The following day the 5/7th Gordons attacked Touffreville. Along with 11 Platoon, we supported them by firing on a strongly-held

---

2. Map Reference 137694.

infantry position on the *Butte de la Hogue*, whereupon sixty to seventy Germans jumped out of their trenches and began running back into the cover of a wood and no more was seen of them. Ten belts per gun, 2,500 rounds, were fired. 12 Platoon also fired four belts per gun at other German MG positions in a wood slightly further south on the *Butte de la Hogue*. The Gordons captured Touffreville in little over half an hour.

Over the next couple of days there were German counterattacks in the form of heavy infiltrations, but these were beaten off by the Gordons.

On 15 June 12 Platoon was ordered to hand over the position to the 2nd Derbyshire Yeomanry and move to a gap in our defences, south of Escoville. Information had been received that there was going to be an attack by the 21st Panzer Division from the direction of Cuverville in the early hours of the following morning. We did not take too much notice of that. It got dark at about 2200 hours and so we waited until then to avoid the Germans seeing us pull out, moved across to this new area along a line of one 17-Pounder and three 6-Pounder anti-tank guns of the 61st Anti-Tank Regiment. The platoon's job was to protect the anti-tank guns, so we dug our 'V' shaped trenches and set up the machine guns.

The four Vickers guns were dug in about ten yards apart, this being close enough to enable any orders to be heard. My gun was in the centre right position and was helping to protect the 17-Pounder, which was about twenty yards to our right. Due to the darkness, no one had any idea what the ground in front was like.

At about 0400 hours, over the brow of a hill the sound of enemy tanks and vehicles could be heard in Cuverville about three miles away. My Number 2 was my old Beretta pistol-wielding mate, Ginger Richardson. He would roll his own cigarettes and keep the makings in an old tin, and whenever things got a bit sticky, he would scramble for this tin. At times I would shout and swear at him, '*Never mind rolling a fag Ginger, get that ammunition coming through!*' To which he would

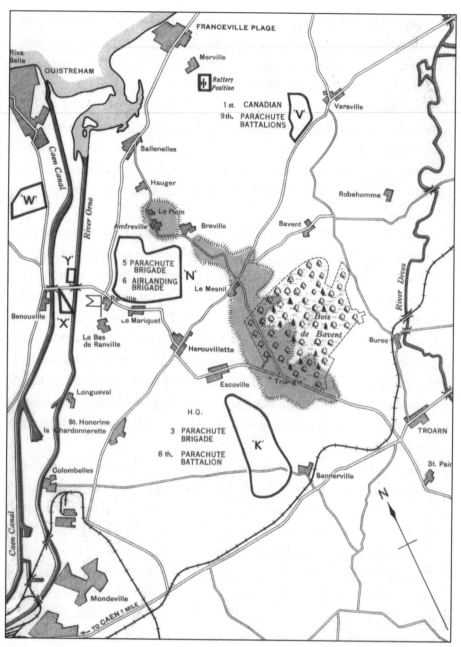

Normandy.

reply, '*If I get captured I'll not be without a fag.*' I kept telling him the first thing the Germans would do was smoke all his fags, but it was no good, he would not change. I tossed a coin to see who would get the first kip. I won, but as I laid down at about 0430 hours, a heavy barrage opened up. Just as I said to Ginger, '*We must be putting an attack in somewhere,*' shells started landing all around us. Then *Nebelwerfers*, fearsome five-barrelled electric projectors that made the most awesome noise when fired, joined in. However, the mortars were the worst problem. During this barrage my stomach felt like lead.

Shortly after it stopped and before it became properly light, the sound of tracked vehicles could be heard approaching from the direction of Cuverville. Their sound got nearer and nearer, until they could eventually be heard on the roadside in front, about 200 yards away. I withheld fire in order not to give our position away and they passed in front, then down the road about 200 yards to our right, finally reaching a crossroads just to the rear, near Escoville. This was defended by 'C' Squadron, 2nd Derbyshire Yeomanry, who opened up heavy direct fire at the enemy vehicles, which halted and then began to withdraw. We did not open fire as we could not see a target, however our artillery *had* fired, one shell scoring a direct hit on one of these vehicles. We thought they were tanks.

It started to get light at around 0500 hours and in front of us a field full of corn about four feet high gradually appeared, parts of which had been set on fire by the exploding shells. Suddenly, out of this smoke and flame appeared panzer grenadiers, shouting, screaming, firing and throwing stick grenades in our direction. We immediately realized that the vehicles had not been tanks but half-tracks carrying these men, who had subsequently crawled through the cornfield. I honestly thought 'This is a bad dream and I'm going to wake up back home in my little bedroom.' I was petrified, but these grenadiers obviously had no idea that there were four Vickers machine guns dug in along the hedgerow. Captain Gibbs shouted '*Gun control!*' so that each gun selected its own target. I opened fire. A few fleeting figures passed by me in the half-light, smoke and cordite which the damp atmosphere was holding close to the ground. I thought 'Christ, they've got through us.' When the Germans I could clearly see were only yards from us, I told myself 'I've got to stop here and hang on because if they get to me, I'm going to be shot. They are not going to take a machine-gunner prisoner who has just been killing all their blokes, and if I get out of this trench to run, they're going to kill me anyway as I'll be in the open field.' As it turned out the figures passing me were a few members of the anti-tank gun crew. I suppose a bloke took to his heels and one or two others followed him. If one person panics, it's easy for it to spread. Within seconds the sergeant in charge of them, a little Scottish fellow, had got them back.

The thing that saved us was a strand of barbed wire about five yards away that the farmer had placed to keep cattle out of the cornfield. The leading grenadiers ran into this and most were held up for a vital few seconds. Nothing could stand up to the direct fire of four Vickers machine guns at that range. The grenadiers dropped in their tracks. The infantry mortars began to plaster the cornfield and we were at rapid-fire non-stop, a belt at a time, so any Germans crawling through the corn must have been slaughtered. I fired eight belts into the cornfield, spraying it all over, four of them helping enemy stragglers to withdraw. However, to the left all three of the smaller anti-tank guns had been knocked out, leaving the 17-Pounder to my side.

Then down the road from Cuverville came six Mk IV tanks, led by an eight-wheeled armoured car. The enemy plan must have been for these grenadiers to destroy the anti-tank guns to allow their tanks to break through. The 17-Pounder fired a round and missed. I thought 'That's a good start.' However, they then proved themselves by knocking out the armoured car, preventing them coming any further down the road. As they were in a sunken road and could not get out of it, the next four shots each destroyed a tank.[3] The grenadiers supporting these tanks went to ground in the road. The officer in the remaining tank climbed out and we could see him walking along the road, appearing to urge them to move forward into our murderous barrage. He was unsuccessful and climbed back onto his tank, but of course many guns targeted him and he did not make it. He must have been a very resolute officer. This tank took refuge in a wood to the right, and as I thought there was bound to be some Germans in this wood, I fired two belts into that. Frank Dollin then came along and asked what I was firing at. I explained and he said, *'Well don't fire at anything you can't see. Save your ammunition.'*

As they could not get through us, the enemy now shifted the direction of their attack to our right and I could hear the four guns of our 11 Platoon hammering away in support of the 1st Gordons. Eventually, the attack was beaten off.

Following an action like that, after being so keyed up, you felt listless, shattered. You could not do anything. I just sat in the trench for a few minutes and my entire platoon was exactly the same, reflecting on what had just happened and the fact that we were still alive. The Vickers gun to my right had been knocked out and all the crew killed by a direct hit from a *Nebelwerfer*. Some *Nebelwerfer* rounds were filled with ball bearings and other bits, and the bloke in charge of the gun had a wound through the back of his head. My own gun was out of action with a bit of mortar shrapnel through the water jacket.

Our RSM was known as 'Rocky' Knight, because we thought he was as stiff as a rock. We did not say that to his face of course. He came up with another gun as we always carried a spare, and we continued to fire at targets for the remainder of the morning.

---

3. After this, being in the same Brigade we often used to bump into that particular anti-tank gun crew of the 91st Anti-Tank Regiment RA. They would see us and say, *'We're alright now you're with us,'* and we would say likewise. They took care of the tanks and we took care of any infantry, so we got quite friendly.

At about two o'clock that afternoon a Gordon Highlander officer came over and said, '*Did you get any of those Germans close up?*' I said, '*Yes, there's one lying out there just in front of us, an officer.*' He was only eight feet in front of our gun. He said, '*I'll get one of my blokes to get his pay book.*' Thinking that being an officer he would have a nice watch [spoils of war], plus his Luger had fallen just in front of him, I said, '*Don't worry, I'll go and get it.*' I said to Ginger, '*You take over the gun and keep an eye on me.*' He said, '*I will but I want half of what you get!*' I said, '*OK, I don't want his watch, I want that gun.*' There were several Germans lying directly out in front and I went over to this officer, who was lying face down, half on his side, spread-eagled, and there was the pistol about three feet in front of his hand. I was stood over and a little in front of him and went to pick the Luger up, when the German launched himself forward to grab it as well! We both missed it. I could not believe what was happening. My revolver was in its holster, buttoned up with the safety catch on, so too late to get it out now. Beside him was his entrenching tool, which he snatched up with the intention of slicing my head off. In desperation I grabbed him, putting my arms around his body to stop him being able to raise the entrenching tool. He was not much bigger than me and I could feel his breath on my cheek. As we were struggling I was shouting out, '*Ginger! Ginger! For Christ's sake shoot him!*' He said, '*I cannae shoot him, man. Yer too close!*' The others were shouting '*Get down*', '*Jump to the left*', '*Jump to the right,*' and I was shouting, '*I can't let go of him!*' This all happened in seconds but I realized I could not hold onto him much longer, so I yelled, '*When I shout 'NOW', I'm going to drop straight down.*' This I did and Corporal Ned Bull immediately shot him with his Sten. I could not rejoin my comrades quickly enough and when I got back to our side of the hedge, the Gordons officer was laughing his head off. He said, '*I thought you two were having a waltz across No Man's Land!*' In my haste I did not get the paybook and said, '*You go and get your own bloody ID. I'm not going out there any more!*'

I never even got the Luger as someone else pinched it. That was my lesson. Do not go looking for souvenirs.

When the Gordons officer went out there with a couple of his blokes, they put a few more rounds in the one I had wrestled with, who was already dead, and then another German got up and he was shot. A third one began to rise and appeared to be on his knees, with his hands in a position as if he was praying for his life. They still shot him, which I thought was not necessary. All were grenadiers of the 21st Panzer Division.

I've often thought about what must have been going through this German officer's mind as he laid there in front, virtually underneath our gun, which was firing three or four feet over the top of him all morning for nine hours or so. It must have been terrible for him, and then to end up getting killed. I don't know why he did not just surrender. Perhaps he thought that succeeding waves would overrun us.

After the Germans had pulled back and things had quietened down, I took some men and had a cautious look around the battlefield. I knew there were no mines because of the Germans having come through the field. In the dip in the road down which the enemy vehicles had passed, I saw two German bodies beside this old, small French tank. They must have been killed some time before because when I turned each of them over, maggots were coming out of the eyes and mouth. I carried on looking around. There was a horrible little bloke in our platoon who was about four feet six inches tall and looked like Mr Punch. I saw him holding a bayonet, crouched over a German body. I said, '*What are you doing Tich?*' and then saw that he was prising a ring off this German's finger. '*What are you doing that for?*' He said, '*I'm not going to leave this war with nothing, like they did after the first war.*' I said, '*Tich, you disgust me. If you get caught with a pocketful of rings, you don't expect to make it to the prisoner of war camp do you?*' He just rambled on, so I pointed out the French tank to him and mentioned the two dead Germans there. I went back and told the rest of the blokes what he had been up to. Tich then came back and said, '*You rotten so and so.*' All I said was, '*Did you get their rings?*' In the end no one would speak to him.[4]

Of the overall situation after the attack, some infiltration was made along the Brigade front, but these positions were eventually cleared up and for the next couple of days there was no German attack. The only real moment of 'excitement' was on 18 June when the Platoon Commander's carrier, which was parked in a sunken road, was hit and caught fire during a barrage. It burned for quite a while, which drew more fire from Jerry. They threw everything at it.

We stayed in that position for about five days and after being relieved by another of our platoons, went to a position just south of the le Mesnil crossroads, we thought for a bit of rest and reorganization, but on 23 June this area was heavily shelled and Frank Dollin was wounded and evacuated.

*   *   *

During the early hours of 1 July, 10 and 12 Platoons, supporting the 5/7th Gordons, were sent forward to relieve the 5th Cameron Highlanders in a village called St Honorine La Chardonerette. We dug in on its southern edge, behind and on the right-hand corner of a very thick wall about six-foot high. The Vickers was not much good in a confined area, so we were always positioned in a location that gave a clear field of fire. It was not like a Bren, which could be swept around and fired from the hip.

Everyone was well dug in. The trenches had the corrugated iron roofs upon which was put the excavated earth. This gave a reasonably safe and dry trench. They certainly saved a lot of casualties from the shrapnel of airburst shells. This was one advantage of having a carrier. All this material, plus the brewing up tin and the cooking bits were strapped to the back of the carriers. We looked like a bunch of rag and

---

4. He does not appear on the casualty list produced after the war, so I don't know what happened to him.

bone men when we drove along! No one was there to tell us we could not have the extra items.

We soon found that this village was a very nasty place, not surprising when it was situated on a forward slope and in a bit of a salient. Consequently, fire was coming from three sides and we were also under observation by the enemy artillery. Each morning, Churchill tanks were brought down to support us, but had to go back at around 2200 hours, as the Germans would pick them off during the night.

The 21st Panzer Division possessed very resolute soldiers. Some of them could speak English and while here, they would approach at night and moan, pretending to be wounded, saying things like, '*My leg, my leg. Help me Mother. Come and get me.*' Of course, if someone fell for it and went out there, they were shot. On other occasions they would taunt us. A voice would come out of the blackness, '*Tommy. Coffee break. We take ten!*' Another favourite was '*Tommy. Have you got a fag?*' If you answered, they would fire a machine pistol at you. However, on occasions we did get our own back. During another night one of them shouted, '*Hey, Tommy. Throw us a fag!*' So someone threw a Mills bomb and answered, '*We haven't got any fags. Have this instead you German bastard!*' Then the voice came back, '*That's not nice, Tommy!*'

Ten days were spent in this position with them around us all night and so we did not get much sleep. There were no major attacks, but on several occasions there were Company-sized assaults across the fields from the various small woods dotted about. However, the Germans never got close enough to get amongst us.

* * *

Elements of the 12th SS *Hitler Jugend* Division had also arrived opposite the Highland Division at Colombelles. Here, a steelworks with two very tall chimneys gave the Germans the ability to observe the entire eastern bridgehead area. These chimneys had to go. First our massed artillery had an attempt but made no impression on them. Then, the following afternoon we had to take cover while a low-level air attack by about fifty twin-engine RAF bombers took place. We watched from our trenches in St Honorine as the smoke and debris gradually cleared to reveal the chimneys still standing. The next idea was for a silent infantry attack to capture and hold this steelworks long enough for the Royal Engineers to blow them up and then withdraw back to our own front line. No fresh infantry were available for the operation, so it was decided to use the 5th Black Watch, which had suffered heavy casualties since its arrival in Normandy and whose men were already tired. To accompany them were eleven Sherman tanks and our 10 Platoon, which was to be moved from St Honorine. The operation began at 0100 hours on 11 July and although a night attack, the defenders heard the Jocks coming. Waiting until they were a few hundred yards away the Germans opened a devastating fire. To complete the nerve wracking situation, at 0630 hours three Tiger and two Mk IV tanks appeared. The Shermans were no match and ten of them were immediately knocked out. The carriers were ordered out, leaving the Middlesex men behind, something the drivers and particularly Dennis Daly were very uncomfortable with. At 0830 hours orders came for our infantry to withdraw to their original positions. Somehow everything was brought back using wheelbarrows and things like that. The Black Watch again suffered grievous losses. The chimneys remained standing.

The whole of the 51st Highland Division had not been trained for European fighting. Everyone was used to desert warfare and having only been back in England for a few months, had not had time for training in close-quarter work in fields and hedgerows. Consequently, the Division had not performed very well since arriving in France. The killing fields of Normandy had been a terrible awakening. The Division had carried out a good number of attacks and suffered heavy casualties, when previously it had been sweeping through the desert. It was very depressing.

*   *   *

By now Captain Gibbs had proved himself to us in 'C' Company. He had turned out to be all right, but we still pulled his leg. When all the shells were flying about, I would say to him *'What's going on?' 'I don't really know,'* he would say. *'But you're the officer, you're supposed to know!'* During this stay in St Honorine the Germans laid a red smoke screen on our position, and Gibbs jumped out of the trench with a Bren gun. I suppose he had recently seen some American war film. I said to him, *'What are you doing?' 'I'm going to have a look at what's in that smoke screen.'* I said, *'For Christ's sake get yourself back in your hole. You'll get yourself hurt.'* He said, *'Do you think so?' 'Think so? I bloody know so!'*

Due to the amount of casualties, the infantry battalions we supported had only stayed in St Honorine for three days before being withdrawn, but as they did not have any machine gunners, we had had to stay there. During the morning of the eleventh day, I was sitting on the edge of my trench when Captain Gibbs said to me, *'Fed up?'* I said, *'Of course I'm fed up. We're all fed up. We've had enough of it. We've been here for ten days, seen three infantry battalions come and go and we're stuck here with no sign of relief. We haven't had a proper meal, just bully beef and biscuits. You're going to wake up one morning and you'll be on your own!'* He said, *'You can't do that Corporal.'* I said, *'You watch us!'* Gibbs went away and returned a little while later. He had been in wireless contact with Battalion Headquarters. *'I've got some good news for you, Corporal.'* I said, *'What's that? Are we being relieved?' 'No, the Colonel is coming down to have a chat with you all at two o'clock this afternoon.'* We all laughed. *'You must be joking! Nothing can move in daylight down that slope into the village.'* Anyway, we did not believe it, but awaited the arrival of two o'clock with interest. Sure enough at the appointed time, over the hill came a jeep driven by Tommy Roberts. I can only assume that the Germans were so surprised that they had to look twice to make out what was happening. Tommy drove down into the village and out jumped Lieutenant Colonel Man. He rubbed his hands together and said, *'Gather round, lads. I'm going to have a talk with you,'* but we would not move away from our trenches. '*Come on, come on. Around me,*' he said. We all reluctantly got out of our slit trenches and stood there. He just had time to say, '*It's a nice spot you've got here. I'd like to fetch my little daughter here for a picnic!*' before we heard the Germans drop their mortar bombs down the barrels, plop, plop, plop. We knew there was about ten seconds before they arrived, so everyone made a dive for our trenches while he was saying, '*Where are you going?*' Someone commented, '*You'll bloody soon find out!*' The mortar bombs began landing and the Colonel dived in the first trench he could find. The bloke whose trench it was, Corporal Bob Burnett had to lay on top of him and got bloody wounded. For twenty minutes the Germans plastered us and blew the Colonel's jeep to bits, although fortunately Tommy was all right. When they finally let up, the Colonel started to run back across the field and up the slope. Only being a short bloke, his legs were going ten to the dozen. Someone shouted out, '*Where are you going Colonel? To fetch your daughter?*' He turned around, shook his fist and said, '*I'll have you bastards!*' Anyway, we were relieved the next day, 14 July, so it did a bit of good![5] [6]

5. Later on, the Colonel said to Tommy Roberts, '*I'm not liked in this Battalion am I?*' Tommy said without thinking, '*No, you're not.*' '*How about you Corporal Roberts, do you like me?*' Before Tommy could stop himself he said, '*No, I don't!*' He said, '*Right. Take me to Headquarters take those two stripes off your arm. You're in a machine-gun crew now.*' So he lost his job, which was much better than being on a machine gun. Actually, Colonel Man was not bad after that. He was quite clever and got promoted. About a year after the war, when I had left the Battalion, a friend of mine Harry Alcock, said that they were in a particular barracks and they had a new CO, who had never been in action, and was finding fault with everything. And so on one occasion he confined everyone to barracks. Colonel Man happened to be in the area and decided to pay a visit to his old battalion. He arrived and said to the guard sergeant, '*Where is everybody? There's no one about,*' so the sergeant told him what had occurred. He said, '*What, all of them?*' '*Yes, the CO's confined them all.*' Colonel Man called this officer and said to him, '*These men have fought and won a war. You do not treat them like this. Pack your bags. I'll be leaving in half an hour, and you'll be coming with me. You're not fit to be in charge of these men.*'
6. Many years later, at a Reunion dinner, I was sitting there talking when Colonel Man burst in through some swing doors and shouted, '*Look out! The old bastard's here!*' I

The platoons arrived in Ranville where there was a Mobile Bath Unit. Everyone got undressed and walked into these marquee-type tents, stark naked, and had a short time in there under the showers. Big lorries were employed to heat the water. On exiting the other end of the tent you were confronted by piles of clothes that had been fumigated and everyone just had to grab what they could, whether it fitted or not. Later on, people could pick someone out who was obviously wearing something that did not fit them but fitted you and exchanged clothes!

* * *

After the shambles of Colombelles, Monty replaced General Bullen-Smith with a Highlander, General Tom Rennie, a change of command that was welcomed by everybody. Morale began to rise and of course the men had learned by their mistakes in the type of fighting required for the Normandy countryside.

At this time I developed an abscess between my legs, where I had previously been wounded, and could hardly walk. After being told that I had to go to hospital because staying would only mean becoming a bloody nuisance, I ended up in Bayeux. In the hospital I felt like a malingerer because there was a wounded soldier in every bed. The beds were very close together and in the one beside me was a Polish tank soldier who was blinded, his head being completely wrapped in bandages. He could not speak any English and so nobody could understand him. After a while he started shouting. All the staff were extremely busy and this shouting went on for ages. I could not guess what he was on about. Suddenly, he pulled the bed sheets back and urinated all over the floor. He had been desperate. I got an orderly, a French women carrying out the cleaning, to come over and clean

---

talked to him later and said, '*What you said wasn't very complimentary, Colonel.*' He said, '*Listen here sergeant, as long as they call me an evil bastard and all the rest of it, I know everything's alright. It's when they start getting polite that I know they're up to something. That's the time I've got to watch out!*'

up. After doing this she asked if I could help to prevent it happening again. So somehow I managed to communicate with him and arrange a system. When he 'wanted the bottle' he shouted '*PISS!*' and when he wanted the bedpan, it was '*SHIT!*' I could hobble about, so I would go and get whatever he needed. I don't know what happened after I was discharged. Perhaps someone took over my job!

Eventually, I was examined and told that I had to have a cyst cut from the rather inglorious position of the cheeks of my backside because they were rubbing together. However, on three occasions when I was due to have it done, it was postponed for more urgent cases coming in. Eventually, I made it clear to the doctor that I felt terrible lying amongst all these wounded, when all I had in effect was a boil on my bum! Shortly after, the doctor found time to attend to me and within a few days I was discharged. All such cases were put on board a truck and driven to a replacement camp. As we entered the camp, I could not believe my eyes. Although not very far behind the front line, there were whitewashed stones everywhere. A flagpole had been erected and everybody was marching around saluting everyone else, their equipment and gaiters all scrubbed. The others went to report in, but I joined the back of a working party that was marching out of the gate and once outside, promptly dropped out. I spent the rest of that day walking. I only had my shaving kit. The first night I slept in an old trench. The next day, after walking for a while, an ambulance came alongside and I flagged it down. I asked if they were going up to the front, which they were, so I scrounged a lift. After a while they stopped, brewed up and gave me something to eat. That night I slept in the ambulance with the crew.

The following morning they had taken me as far as they could and I got out and started walking again. Shortly after, to my surprise a truck with an HD marking came along. I realized from the number, 87, that it was from Divisional Headquarters, so I flagged it down because I knew some Middlesex Regimental personnel would be there. Upon arrival, a Jock officer, who looked at me rather strangely as I had not had a wash or shave in a few days, told me where to find the Middlesex. On my way there, I ran straight into RSM 'Rocky' Knight! Seeing the state of me, he exploded. *'What are you doing here?'* I said, *'I won't tell you a lie, I've just come out of hospital and didn't like what I saw at the replacement camp, so I walked out and here I am.'* He said, *'Do you know you're classed as a deserter?'* I said, *'Well I'm deserting in the wrong direction aren't I?'* However, his attitude had changed and he asked if I had had any breakfast. I said, *'No, I've had nothing for two days really.'* He said, *'Come with me!'* I followed him to the cookhouse. The cook was a Sergeant Bowden, a miserable old so-and-so. The RSM said, *'Cook this corporal some breakfast.'* *'Breakfast has finished.'* *'Cook him some breakfast. Double rations.'* He gave me the lot, including egg, bacon, tinned tomatoes, bread and butter and a big mug of tea. I was then to have a wash and shave and report back to him.

While I had been away, Colonel Man had been promoted and posted elsewhere. The replacement was his Second-in-Command, formerly Major, now Colonel Parker, who was a much more easy-going chap. The RSM subsequently marched me in to see him. The CO said, *'What's all this? Do you know you are classed as a deserter?'* I said, *'I was going the right way Colonel.'* He answered, *'We could do with a few more coming this way.'* Then after explaining what I had done, he ordered the Sergeant Major to *'Take him out and then come back in.'* I was marched out and the RSM said, *'When I take you back in, tell him you were returning to your unit and lost your papers.'* I was marched back in. Colonel Parker said, *'You're a fine sort of a corporal aren't you?'* *'I don't understand, Colonel.'* *'You were discharged from hospital back to unit and you've lost your papers! That's not very good for a corporal is it?'* I said, *'I was in such a hurry to come back that I forgot to pick them up!'* He said, *'All right. Glad to see you back,'* and arranged for me to return to my Company. Colonel Parker knew when to turn a blind eye and we found him to be a first class officer.

Later that day I arrived back at the Company. 'Lofty' Pearson greeted me with *'You're just in time. We're going to do an attack tonight! But*

firstly, I am promoting you to sergeant and you are going to 10 Platoon.'
I said, *'I'd sooner stop where I was.'* He said, *'You're going. Don't argue
with me and I won't ask how you got back here.'* So in a few hours I was
going into an attack with a platoon I did not know. With 12 Platoon I
had supported the 5/7th Gordons right through the desert (although
I did get 'loaned out' at times). Joining 10 Platoon meant that I now
supported the 5th Black Watch.

The Company Commander had the authority to promote people on
the spot. He would inform the Colonel, but the paperwork could take
days or even weeks to come through. At first you were acting unpaid
sergeant for six months [a corporal was acting unpaid for three months].
Within that three or six months the majority would either be killed or
made a casualty and never did get paid for being a sergeant. After six
months you became what was known as 'War Substantiated'. You got
quite a bit of extra money for being a machine-gunner, threepence a
day, and as a War Substantiated Sergeant, ten shillings and tenpence a
day, but then I had to pay income tax on it because I was single. This
was called Post-War Credits and I was stopped tenpence a day![7]

I found my new platoon and introduced myself. The Platoon
Commander was Captain Roderick MacPherson, a fiery, ginger-headed
Scotsman. My new driver was Tommy Tubbs, a very likable chap, who
I found would never complain, whatever situation I got him into. He
would roll his eyes at me sometimes, but nothing ever ruffled him.

People were shifting around to take the place of casualties. A carrier
driver could be told to drive anybody although he did have his own
carrier. It might be out of action for a mechanical reason and so they
could be asked to drive another. Although 10 Platoon was assigned to
support the 5th Black Watch, as usual we could be moved to support
other battalions when required, and likewise the other Middlesex
platoons could come to us.

---

7. It was thirteen years after the war before the Government paid me back. I received
   thirteen pounds.

That night, on 7 August, we took part in an attack to finally capture Caen. Beforehand we were given earplugs because the area immediately in front was heavily bombed. Following this, 10 Platoon supported the attack from a place called Ifs, just south of Caen and east of the River Orne. At 2330 hours all of the platoons commenced firing on a specific wood south of Tilly la Campagne. The fire programme was three belts per gun on a range of 3,950 yards. Fifteen minutes later, we switched to another wood and the road junction at Secqueville la Campagne, again three belts per gun in eight minutes at 3,800 yards. Then at 0008 hours we switched back to the initial wood target for two minutes rapid fire. There was no response from the enemy. Two battalions of 152 Brigade then advanced towards Tilly la Campagne. At 0022 hours our fire was switched to the area of La Hogue; two belts rapid fire. Twenty minutes later, we switched back to our second target wood. This was again typical of the kind of work we were used for. 154 Brigade then began to advance. It was their task to pass through Tilly and consolidate at a crossroads just to the south. With the enemy mostly fighting rearguard actions, we were able to advance a considerable distance in some places, but when it became light it was found that we had lost contact with the Black Watch. Captain MacPherson, together with a dispatch rider went forward to regain contact. After a short while the dispatch rider returned telling me to follow him with our six carriers immediately, and as we were under sporadic fire, he shot off along the road and disappeared in a cloud of dust. I reached a 'Y' Junction and Tommy said, '*Which way?*' He knew I didn't know, but if you show hesitation you are lost. It seemed there were shells falling to the right, so I said, '*Go right.*' After about half a mile, on rounding a bend we were greeted by the sight of a 60-ton Tiger tank completely blocking the road. I have never seen six carriers disappear in such a short time! However, for some reason it had not fired at us, so I cautiously approached on foot, making a big detour. I found that although the front of the tank was intact, the rear had been hit by a rocket-firing Typhoon. Shortly after, we caught up with the Black Watch.

During the early evening 153 Brigade attacked Secqueville la Campagne but there was little opposition. We stopped at a farmhouse for the night.

On 18 August, 10 Platoon supported the Black Watch crossing of the River Dives at St Pierre-sur-Dives then through St Marie-aux-Anglais to Grandcamp, passing a Chateau on the left. We turned right through a large dog-breeding kennels. Immediately passing the farthest building, I saw the Commanding Officer of the 5/7th Gordons, Lieutenant Colonel Blair-Imrie and three other men lying on the ground. As I dismounted it became apparent that all four men were dead. I could not wait about as we had to reach our infantry who were storming a saddle of hills that completely overlooked our line of advance, but just as I was about to climb back into the carrier a German soldier came out of a bush a few yards away and surrendered, shouting that he was Polish. We searched him, then about fifteen of his comrades who had been watching, also appeared and surrendered. They all claimed to be Poles, saying that they had fired over our heads. When I asked who had killed the four Jocks, each claimed that it was not him. At this stage, out of nowhere an Army Padre appeared in a jeep. He asked what was going on. I said, 'We don't know what to do with these prisoners as we have to go forward.' One of my men said, although not seriously, 'Shoot the bastards.' The Padre said, 'You can't shoot prisoners,' and offered to lead them to the rear. They must have got the gist of the conversation and were only too happy to fall in behind his jeep.

We proceeded up the slope, but this became so acute that our tracks could not get a firm grip, so the guns and ammunition were unloaded and carried to the top in the blazing sunshine. Arriving at the top of the crest, the reverse slope turned out to be all scrubland and we could not see a thing, so everything had been carried up there for nothing. The platoon stayed at this spot for the remainder of the day and following night.

The next morning we moved forward to St Pierre-des-Ifs and then the Brigade's final objective of Lisieux, which was liberated after three days of hard fighting. Then the breakout really began, moving into the Mauny loop of the River Seine, with the infantry taking hundreds of prisoners. German barges ferrying troops across the river provided excellent targets for our machine guns. Their transport was parked, waiting to get across.

After crossing the Seine at Elboeuf, it was on to Rouen, where a tumultuous welcome awaited us. The streets were full of waving, laughing people, trying to give us bottles of plonk. The fighting had moved on, but we then went to St Valery, the site of the original 51st Highland Division's epic stand in 1940, to spend a few days being feted by the villagers.

* * *

The next objective was the capture of Le Havre, a part of the Atlantic Wall, with very strong fortifications. To reach Le Havre our route had to pass through the Forest of Montegon, and while approaching it during the night of 9 September, we were to meet a member of the local French Resistance, a man of about twenty years of age, who would guide us through it along the tracks. This was ideal as it could have been very disorientating trying to get through a forest at night. This man duly completed his task successfully, but afterwards he would not leave. It was explained to him that not being a trained soldier he would get in the way, but he said, '*No. I want to come and kill Germans!*' So in the end we told him to keep quiet and he came with us.

In the early hours of the following morning the Highland Division together with the 49th Division began their attempt to capture the port.

On the outer edge of the forest there was a bit of a road that led in the direction of Le Havre. The column set off and my carrier was the eighth vehicle from the front. Ahead was a mixture of tanks, self-propelled guns and armoured cars. The progress of the column was slowed as it began to run into various unmarked mined areas and gradually the vehicles in front were knocked out one after the other.

Finally, when the self-propelled 17-Pounder in front got hit, I found myself in the unenviable position of being the leading vehicle! Shortly after taking over the lead of the column, ahead I could see massive fortifications, blockhouses. That lead feeling in my stomach returned. I said to my driver, '*Christ, how on earth are we going to get near them?*' I stopped the carrier and immediately a Yeomanry regiment armoured car drove up from behind. The officer got out, came up to me and asked why I had stopped and I told him there was a minefield ahead that had not been swept. He said, '*Well my tanks are down there.*' I assured him that they were not down the road because I was the leading vehicle. However, he insisted that he'd had a message from them and that they were down that road. I knew they were not. His vehicle was behind Tommy Tubbs' carrier, which was immediately behind me. We had got there without encountering any mines and he had in effect driven up in our tracks. The officer said, '*Move over and let me go by.*' I said, '*It hasn't been swept.*' So he said, '*Get one of your carriers to drive around you, and if he doesn't get blown up, I know I'll be alright. It's worth losing one carrier to find out.*' I thought 'Yeah, but not bloody mine.' Tommy wasn't too happy! So I got everyone else off the carrier and said, '*I'm sorry Tommy.*' He then drove off the road and into the minefield, but nothing happened. The armoured car then followed the same route, got back onto the road and after proceeding about twelve yards, blew up on a Teller mine. The officer had been injured in the head and was shouting, '*I'm deaf, I'm deaf, I can't hear a thing.*' I pulled the driver out. He had lost both legs and subsequently died. If I had not stopped and he had not gone around me, that would have been my fate.

The REs eventually came up to clear the road and at this point I heard the noise of approaching aero engines and 300 four-engined bombers started carpet bombing. To my surprise the enemy soldiers started to leave their fortifications and run towards us to surrender. They must have thought they would be safe with us. They certainly had more faith in the accuracy of the RAF than we did. That was how we got through the first lot of blockhouses.

Afterwards, after advancing again we captured an enemy 88mm anti-aircraft site, where most of the defenders had been killed by the bombing raid. We were not needed to take part in the final mopping up, so I entered one of the dugouts. It was full of dead *Luftwaffe* personnel, all killed by concussion. Many of them were still sitting around a table. They all had mucus coming out of their ears and nose. I took the pay books from seven of them. When I came out an officer that I did not know appeared and I mentioned the pay books to him. He said, '*Can I see the bodies of these Germans?*' I don't know why, perhaps he thought we had shot them. After seeing the bodies, I asked him if he wanted me to pull them out, but he said, '*No, I don't think so.*'

The Highland Division eventually ended up capturing 122 officers and 4,500 other ranks. The number of enemy casualties was not known.

While here, the Black Watch discovered a German Quartermaster's store, which included booze. The guard they put around it was stronger than Monty's HQ! There were some very happy Black Watch, Middlesex and one French Resistance boy until the MPs arrived.

Chapter Nine

Holland and Germany

The Company was now rested near Etretat, about fifteen miles north of Le Havre. It was in the middle of nowhere. Here, there were a lot of parades and inspections courtesy of our RSM to show that he was still in charge. During this period the Arnhem operation, *Market Garden* commenced. All our wheeled transport was taken to carry supplies up the corridor. After about two weeks the vehicles returned and we prepared for our next operation. The result of *Market Garden* was an Allied corridor that stretched through to the Nijmegen area.

On 28 September our move towards Holland began, travelling via Rierux and Berlaar, and arriving on the road between Eindhoven and Nijmegen, on 1 October. 10 Platoon took up position to the west of the town of St Odenrode, firing on fixed lines in front of the 5th Black Watch. Neither side had the troops to do anything substantial, so we only held the road and pieces on either side, while the Germans fired across the road at supply lorries going to and fro from Nijmegen and beyond. The platoons could be called out to wherever this had occurred on the road and when the Germans started firing again, everyone had to immediately jump into their carriers, mount the guns and fire back. On top of this, aggressive German patrols were continually breaking through our defence of this supply line, so we had to sleep fully clothed, ready for instant action. At one particular spot where they came over, we positioned our machine guns in front of a Dutch farmhouse, opened fire and of course the Germans fired back. On subsequent occasions when the Germans came this way again, as soon as we arrived the Dutch family would run out and sit around the other side of the house to avoid the incoming German fire! On another occasion a convoy of RASC lorries drove up the road and came under fire. They all jumped out of the trucks and into the ditches. I walked over to them and an officer got out of the ditch and asked what was going on. I said, '*It's just a few Germans getting a bit saucy. We'll soon sort them out.*' He didn't know what to do, so I told him that as soon as they had passed us, his journey should be all right and so to get his men mounted again and set off. They did this without any subsequent problem. That was typical of what was going on and what we had to do.

My crew was billeted in a house owned by a Dutch lady. In it was an old iron stove that defied all our attempts to light it, so I went outside and syphoned some petrol from the carrier tank into a tin. I put this petrol on the stove and threw in a match. Of course the stove went up! Above it was a mantelpiece that had a cover with tassels and they were all burnt off. The lady came running in and began doing her nut. Never mind about me being a sergeant, she chucked us all out! We found another billet, but I did not try lighting any more stoves with petrol.

Many of the Dutch were very strict in their way of life. In another billet we were playing cards on the table for money. The owner, an old farmer said, '*Not in my house. Stop or get out.*'

At midnight on 22/23 October, the anniversary of El Alamein, Operation *Colin* began for the 51st Highland Division. This was an attempt to clear the area southwest of s'Hertogenbosch, and was part of a general attack that aimed to clear the province of Brabant and the region around the Scheldt river. Besides the Highland Division, the 7th Armoured, 15th Scottish and 53rd Welsh Divisions were also involved, forming 12 Corps. For us it started at a place called Erde. The Divisional objective was the River Maas. At 0100 hours the 5/7th Gordons attacked Wijbosch. Prior to this, in preparation each Vickers gun within the Company had fired 27 belts (6,750 rounds) of ammunition. There was heavy skirmishing, with the Germans defending crossroads, bridges and suchlike. It was daylight when the first main village, Schijndel, was liberated. Sometime after 1500 hours we were standing at a crossroads when there was a sudden burst of *Schmeisser* fire. A Black Watch officer said, '*Where did that come from?*' Someone identified a particular house with a thatched roof. I never saw where it came from, so I don't know if it was correct, but the officer pulled out a Very pistol and fired into the roof and the whole house caught fire. Shortly afterwards, the villagers came back, including a woman whose house it was. Seeing the house on fire, she collapsed. I felt so embarrassed, so guilty. I hoped we could move away quickly.

With the 5th Black Watch we moved west, reaching the River Dommel, south of s'Hertogenbosch. The Germans had destroyed the original crossing, so the Engineers built a Bailey Bridge. Having constructed the sections beforehand, they would arrive at a river and just roll them across and complete the bridge in very quick time.

The next day, after heavy fighting, we entered Esch, about ten miles west of where we set out with the 5th Black Watch.

The platoon was working with the 2nd Seaforths when a breakthrough was made during another night attack. The advance then moved all the way to Vught, which was captured on 26 October by the 7th Black Watch. Vught possessed the only German concentration camp in the Netherlands.[1] I visited this camp shortly after. The advance had been so rapid that the camp guards had not been able to get away. They wore a different uniform, this being a lighter colour to the *Wehrmacht*. A request was made for a prisoner who could speak any English to help in the camp. An inmate called Jerry Verschuren, a chap of about twenty years of age, came forward. He told us that he had been a member of the Dutch Resistance and had twice faced execution by firing squad. They had been taken just up the road at the side of the camp where there was a big half-circle pit, with high ground all around. When it

---

1. Vught concentration camp has been kept as it was and is now a memorial and museum.

came to the moment, each time the Germans shot only some of them, then took the 'reprieved' back to try to get them to talk.[2]

The camp was divided into four sections; one for Jewish prisoners before transit to a camp in Poland, one for Dutch and Belgian Resistance people and political prisoners, another for women and finally one for short-period detainees. The SS (including SS women) guarded the political prisoners with their usual cruelty. The place had its own gallows.

In one building I saw a type of stone sink about six feet long and twelve inches wide, with a runaway. This had apparently been used to cut up people for experiments. Just in front I counted six ovens. Metal stretchers on wheels were used to push the bodies into the ovens. This was done with a long metal rod that had a 'U' on the end that wrapped around the back of the neck.

There were not many wearing these lighter uniforms that reached a prisoner of war camp.

When it was time for us to move on, Jerry Verschuren's home, which was at a place called Malden, near Limburg, was still in the occupied part of Holland and so he did not know what to do. We suggested that he came with us as he could also speak good German, and so after getting Major Pearson to confirm it, he was attached to us an interpreter. In the end Jerry was provided with a uniform, made an honorary sergeant and stayed with us until the end of the war.[3]

*   *   *

The advance west continued and together with the Black Watch, Haaren was occupied. The Middlesex Vickers were used in much the same way as had been the case in North Africa. Depending on the

---

2. A huge monument has been built over this pit featuring the names of many of those executed there.
3. After the war, Major Carter went out of his way to find Jerry, and did so successfully. He subsequently came to all of the Reunions.

situation, the leading infantry company would go into such a village and if the Jocks ran into something that could not be sorted out with their Brens and infantry weapons, or if they wanted to disengage, we would be called forward to put our machine-gun fire wherever they required it. Normally, the guns were taken off the carriers and carried in. We were usually very close behind them and that was the most efficient way of using the Vickers.

On 29 October, Kartsheuvelle was reached with the 5/7th Gordons. There must have been shortage of Forward Observation Officers because 'Lofty' Pearson decided that an OP was required. He therefore ordered a signaller, Ken Thiis, a bloke of Norwegian extraction, and myself to go up to the tower of the town's St. Joseph's Church. Ken positioned his carrier beneath the tower and we carried his receiver up to the top and dropped a wire down to the wireless set that was on board. Unfortunately, we must have been spotted because all of a sudden an armour piercing shell came through the top of the tower, just above our heads. These shells are so quick, you cannot see them coming. If you were looking at the actual gun that fired it, the flash might be visible, but all you could hear was a SWOOSH! Then it was gone, too late to worry about it. Shortly after, another one came through the side of the tower, about knee-high, just missing my legs. Ken said, '*I think it's bloody time we got out of here!*' We could not see what had fired at us and didn't wait to have a look after the second round! It was obviously from a tank or an SP gun.

That night, we slept in an abandoned farmhouse. Our Platoon Commander, Captain Macpherson, chose to sleep in the only bed. During the night an enemy shell hit the roof, causing a heavy chandelier to fall on his head and kill him.[4]

By the end of the month Operation *Colin* was complete and the area south of s'Hertogenbosch was finally clear of Germans. There

4. Captain Macpherson is buried in Bergen-op-Zoom War Cemetery.

was then a short break in operations during which we just rested and cleaned the guns, this being pretty much the same operation as for a rifle. There was a piece of gauze on a string that had a lead weight attached to one end. The barrel was upended and the weight dropped through the barrel. Then it was pulled through and it cleaned off most of the residue that had stuck to the rifling. This was done now and again, but actually cleaning and maintaining the barrel using a piece of four by two flannelette and oil was often performed.

We were billeted on another farm, in a cow byre. This was attached to the main house as the heat from the animals helped to warm it. We were able to get undressed and bed down in the straw. The family had a lovely daughter, Nelly, who was about twenty years of age. One morning when most of us had already got up, Harry Alcock surfaced just as she entered the byre through the kitchen door. Harry was only wearing a shirt, so I grabbed him round the waist and Ned Bull lifted up his shirt and called out 'Nelly!' She looked round, paused and said dismissively, '*More I have seen!*' Poor old Harry. It took quite a while for him to live that down.

In every barrel there are a few rotten apples and I had met only one. A carrier driver who I will only refer to as 'F' was transferred to my platoon against my wishes as previously, during the move into the Airborne corridor he had deserted. He was brought back after being arrested in a cinema in Antwerp. I can understand someone being frightened, but he was a braggart. He had no friends because a friend is to be relied upon in times of need.

To compound matters, almost immediately, Captain Macpherson's replacement arrived and turned out to be the most objectionable martinet that anyone could wish to meet, with a batman to match. One of the English Newspapers had a cartoon with such a character called 'Blutch' and we gave this nickname to our unpopular officer. Later, we adopted a most ugly dog and called it 'Blutch', so if we wanted to say anything about this officer, we would appear to be talking about or to the dog. He never twigged it. His batman knew, but it was more than his life was worth to inform on us.

* * *

On 4 November the aptly named Operation *Guy Fawkes* began in order to clear a twenty-four square mile area west of s'Hertogenbosch, which was virtually enclosed between the Aftwaterings Canal and the River Maas.

Our part in this was an attack on the canal, again supporting the 5th Black Watch, at first light. During the previous afternoon 10 Platoon, individually and at intervals, had to cross two miles of open fields leading to the built-up canal bank. Using rope, the machine guns were hung down our backs, as were the tripods, so that they could not be seen, thereby deceiving the Germans into believing that we were solely infantry moving up. We were to dig into the bank and stay there all night. Why we could not have just moved up during the night, I do not know. At Zero Hour the next morning, our task was to protect eight tanks plus two 'Crocodile' flame-throwing tanks, together with the infantry, after they left the wood behind us and headed for the canal. After reaching the canal bank, between them the 'flaming Crocodiles' would create a path through which the Black Watch would cross in canvas assault boats. Meanwhile, we were to throw our mounted machine guns on top of the bank and open fire on the Germans at the sluice gates in order to stop them being blown up and thereby flooding the surrounding area.

First light arrived and up came the tanks, only to find that they could not get up the bank because it was too steep. The Crocodiles threw some flame across and fortunately it was not a very wide canal. The Black Watch were across in no time, successfully capturing the lock gates. We walked across them and carried the guns to Nieuwkurk, where they were set up while waiting for the carriers to arrive.

The quantity of ammunition required to be used on the lock gates had been carefully calculated and along with the other drivers I had ordered Driver 'F' to fetch up four belts. He was the only one who never reached us, so we were 1000 rounds short. Afterwards, Driver 'F' was found lying in a disused slit trench. He said he had '*Got lost*' but could not explain how he managed to do so while following us in broad daylight. He almost begged me to charge him, but I thought 'No. You can do the same as everyone else. Why should you sit the war out in a military prison while daily, the rest of us are putting our lives on the line?'

The following morning, after a Class 40 Bailey Bridge was brought up, the carriers crossed over and the gun teams took up position in Hoogemaasdijk. During the night, the road tracks were so boggy that every carrier bellied down in the mud. The next day, the platoon was eventually relieved by the 7th Armoured Division whose tanks pulled each carrier out of the mud.

On reaching the River Maas near Huesden, a small village that was almost an island itself, it became apparent that an appalling tragedy had taken place. Artillery fire had opened up on the area and the civilians had asked the Germans where they would be safe from the shelling. The Germans assured them they would be safe in the Town Hall, which was a solid building that incorporated a 130-foot tower. Consequently about 170 civilians, more than ten per cent of the population, had taken refuge in the cellars within it. The day before, the Germans had carried boxes of explosives into the building and when asked if they were going to blow it up, denied it. Only hours before the 5th Camerons reached the village, the explosives were detonated and the tower collapsed onto the building, killing 134 people, 74 of which were children aged sixteen or under. The building was on the western edge of the river and the Germans said that it would give the British observation across the river and over their area. Perhaps events happened more quickly that the Germans expected, but whoever was in charge was callous.

*   *   *

To the east, the Germans had launched a major assault on the US 7th Armoured Division, which was under command of the British Second Army, and although the attack had been halted, the Germans retained a bridgehead on the west bank of the Maas. The Highland Division was ordered to the Weert area, about fifteen miles southeast of Eindhoven. This was the junction between the British and American sectors, which was held by the US 7th Armoured Division. The HD task was to push the Germans back beyond another section of the Aftwaterings Canal and the Zig Canal. It was terribly wet and the ground was sodden. This made it impossible to dig in. Over the next few days the platoons rotated in their fire support of the Jock positions. The enemy artillery fire was heavy and the mud appalling. We crossed the canal on 18 November, but the advance was slow due to mines and artillery fire. However, the German bridgehead was gradually reduced and we were eventually relieved by the Manchesters.

A week later we moved to an area just north of Nijmegen to relieve the American 101st Airborne Division, which had been there since the drop for *Market Garden*. Again, the whole area was flooded and only the raised roads were above water. The Americans were going to send a party of tanks to guide us in. An advance party was formed of two Middlesex carriers, those of Frank Dollin and myself, and he was in charge. Just before leaving, there had been an issue of spirits, a bit of Dutch courage. I had a bottle of gin. Being the junior sergeant I never got the whisky! While driving up the road, five Americans approached us on a truck. We stopped, got out and Frank said to us, '*Don't forget you're British.*' Everyone shook hands and I said to the Yanks, '*Do you want a drink?*' One said, '*Best leave that stuff alone up here.*' I thought 'Well we have come from Alamein. We do know a little bit about such things.' The Germans must have seen this meeting going on because the 'plop, plop, plop,' of their mortars was heard and all the Yanks threw themselves to the ground. Frank hissed at us forcefully '*Stand still! Stand upright!*' Of course, we were crapping our pants but remained standing on the road. The mortar bombs dropped pretty close. Frank then stood over the American in charge and said, *'Have you lost something old chap?'* The Yank said, *'What the hell are you talking about fella?'* Frank said, *'I thought you had dropped something and were looking for it!'*

They then took us in to where they were positioned. The Yanks were all ready, waiting to go. I could not blame them for that, but when we relieved our own blokes, they did not depart until you had actually taken their place in the trench. You would be told to 'watch a certain spot', 'don't do this', 'there's a sniper who's got something covered', that type of thing. The Yanks boarded their trucks and were away. I just managed to stop the last one and ask, *'Where are the Germans then?'* He said, *'Over thar!'* and they were gone. Later on, our obnoxious officer came up with the rest of the platoon and said, *'What do you know?'* I said in an American drawl, *'I can tell you where the Germans are. They're over thar!'* He said, *'Have you been drinking that bottle of gin?'* I said, *'That's what the Yanks told me. It covers half the world.'*

We were actually in an area known as 'The Island' or 'Butunne' because it was between the Rivers Waal and Neder-Rijn (because the Rhine changes its name at that point).

The following morning after the infantry came up, it was decided to send a patrol along the road. Almost immediately a burst of firing was heard. None of our men returned. They were all were captured.

Only the pieces of 'high' ground could be occupied and even then there were no deep trenches as such. To compensate, the Yanks had built a defensive wall, like a stockade, with full boxes of K rations! There were loads of these boxes about and to us it was incredible. K rations were all good grub. There was biscuits, coffee, tins of meat, which was much better than the Bully we were fed! The Dutch had had to leave the area pretty quick, so there were also plenty of pigs, chickens and other livestock about, so it was Christmas dinner each day.

Our cook there was a bloke called Charlie Winthrop, who came from the border area of Cumbria and Scotland. He had been a miner in a shaft that went out under the sea and he would always say, '*I'm never going back to that.*' He cooked our food on a stand upon which sat three large dixies. Beneath it a blower projected a flame that heated these dixies. It was lit by paraffin. This made a lot of noise and when the Germans put over a barrage, poor old Charlie could not hear the shells and mortar bombs coming over. We would get two or three seconds warning and could take cover, but he only knew after the explosions, and his nerves were now going. I therefore spoke to my old friend, Major Alan Carter, now second in command of the Company, about him being in a bad way. Alan said he would try and get a replacement to give him a few days rest. The following night his replacement arrived in a three-tonner that brought up the rations. After delivering the food, Major Carter, driven by RSM 'Rocky' Knight, took Charlie back on that same truck. This vehicle had a canvas back and a metal cab that had a hole through which you could talk to the people in the back. On their journey they had to cross the Nijmegen Bridge, which the Germans had accurately targeted, so the orders were that nothing was to stop on it in order to prevent traffic building up. As they were crossing a German shell hit the steel structure of the bridge, sending shrapnel all around. Later, the RSM explained what had happened. '*I opened the gap in the cab and said '"Are you all right in the back?" but there was no answer.*' Of course, they could not stop and when they did manage to, found that Charlie had been killed by a piece of shrapnel.[5]

---

5. This always bothered Alan that he had sent him back and been subsequently killed. After the war he was determined to find out where he was buried but was unable to do so. He searched everywhere without any luck. He rang me about it and I mentioned that although they used to be Regimental cooks, they all had to go into the Army Catering Corps. Perhaps at the time he was registered with the ACC. Happily, when he got back to the CWGC and mentioned the ACC, he was found straight away. Charlie died on the 4th December 1944 and is buried in grave 1.E.1 in the Jonkerbos War Cemetery near Nijmegen. During the fighting, this was a farm owned by the Jonkerbos family, and a Field Dressing Station was positioned there. And consequently, a lot of badly wounded soldiers eventually died and were buried in this field. After the war, the authorities wanted to move the bodies to a war cemetery, but

About a week into December, during the early afternoon there was a loud explosion and subsequent black smoke. The Germans had blown the Lek dyke. We knew that this could occur at any time and a contingency plan was in place. Operation *Noah* was instigated, each unit having been given a specific time to withdraw, as everyone had to cross the Nijmegen Bridge. We noticed the water slowly rising until it covered the roads completely. When it became dark we could only judge where the road was by keeping station on the telegraph poles to our left. Major Pearson was up and down the column providing advice to everyone, and for us it all went very smoothly.

*   *   *

The battalion went into billets in the s'Hertogenbosch area and everyone thought that would be it for the winter, a comfortable billet and a nice rest. Then the Germans struck the Americans in the Ardennes. It was decided to send XXX Corps to the Ardennes and on Christmas Day we were ordered to move to Liege. It was bitterly cold. With our carriers having steel tracks, they slid across the frozen cobble-stoned roads of Holland and Belgium. I now had Dennis Daly as my driver and going through one town, looking ahead I could see a Yank standing in a doorway with his arms round a Belgian lady, so I said to Dennis, '*Give him a wake-up call.*' Dennis gave the steering a shove and the carrier swung towards them. He saw us coming and jumped out the way. We were a rotten lot!

The Company settled in position on the River Maas between Liege and Namur and began preparing defences. After having been in this position for a while, during a quiet moment when Dennis was not about, Fred Addison and I decided to give carrier driving a bit of a try.

---

these Dutch people created an uproar, stating that '*This was where they died. We want to keep them here.*' They were told that they could not because it was not consecrated ground. However, after an awful lot of argument the ground was consecrated and turned into the Jonkerbos War Cemetery.

The carriers did not have many controls, just the basic gear lever and steering wheel. They did not even have a brake, just an accelerator! The vehicle was brought to a halt by stopping the tracks; they stopped, you stopped. Eventually. This required a bit of space, so of course all the carriers had their front and back track covers missing! I pushed the starter button and drove off down a hill. As we reached the bottom, the side of the field continued to slope down, and as I went to turn the carrier round, it hit some ice and I could not stop it sliding. The carrier slid off the road and ended up in the field. We were very fortunate because they overturned very easily. This field was so icy and the slope so steep that we could not get back onto the road. What we did not know was that an order had been given to move, and Fred and I were missing. Someone must have seen us disappear with the carrier because shortly after, a search party arrived. They went back and found a Bath Unit, because they had big Scammell trucks and one of these subsequently pulled us out and back up the slope. Luckily, there was no comeback, apart from costing us a bottle of whisky. Mind you, Fred was senior to me, so he was in charge! We did not attempt to drive any more carriers.

On 7 January we moved forward in a counter offensive. Concentrating at Marche our job was the left hand of a pincer movement to meet up with the American Army in the area of the Le Roche-en-Ardennes. There was nothing but snow. It was six feet deep and only infantry could move across it. The machine guns could not be fired because after a while the vibration of the gun just made it disappear into the snow.

It was so cold that every piece of clothing we owned was worn. There had also been an issue of a type of windproof, waterproof boiler suit that zipped up and fur-lined leather jackets without sleeves. Generally, the Germans were worse off because they did not have any winter clothing. Many of them were glad to surrender before they froze to death. As an example of just how cold it was, one night, the crew of a 2nd Derbyshire Yeomanry tank decided to park beside us and sleep in their vehicle. Next morning, all four men were found frozen to death.

The tracks of our carriers froze to the ground overnight, so petrol had to be poured over them and the tracks set alight. The driver then jumped in and quickly drove off before catching fire themselves! In the end the carriers had to be changed for four-wheeled drive vehicles with snow chains.

At this time I received a message to report to the Company Office. Thinking, 'What have I done now?' I went up and saw 'Lofty' Pearson. He said, '*I've got some news for you. You're going on leave.*' This was in the middle of the Ardennes Offensive! Leave started when you actually arrived back in England because it could take any length of time to get home from wherever you were. I had ten days leave. It was all very organized. So many would be chosen from the Division at any one time. Initially, you had to go to a Transit Camp. Then the Service Corps would take you to the next stage and so on. Another bloke came with me who lived in Homerton, near Hackney. I stayed with my younger sister in Barnet and so would travel down and go out drinking with him as he knew his way around there. I spent most of my ten days drinking.

By the time I returned to the unit, the Highland Division task had been completed.

In early February the Division was transferred to the First Canadian Army for Operation *Veritable*, the capture of the area between the Rivers Maas and Rhine. Before moving up, for security purposes all of the Divisional signs on the vehicles had to be over-painted. Also, our jackets had to be turned inside out so that no insignia could be seen. The move began on a Sunday and everyone was out walking. We kept stopping as we crossed Holland and all the Dutch people were saying, '*Good luck tomorrow, Jock!*'

At around 0500 hours on 9 February 1945, from the area of Grossbeck, massive fire was opened on enemy positions. Included in this, the 1/7th and 2nd Middlesex machine gun battalions lined up together, their 72 Vickers guns firing 7,200,000 rounds of ammo, all on selected targets to keep Jerry's head down. We fired our 10,000 rounds and then had to change the barrel due to the rifling wearing out.

In front of us was a field that sloped down for a few hundred yards until it reached a stream. This was the border with Germany. Some of our blokes were down there with a few German prisoners building a ford across the stream. They all had very red necks due to the rain and where their collars had been rubbing.

Advancing with the 5th Black Watch, we entered the western tip of the Reichswald near Grafwegen to be greeted by a scene of utter devastation, with German dead and wounded everywhere. Apparently, a *Wehrmacht* Division was being relieved by a Parachute unit when the barrage started and there were a lot more men on the roads and in the open than there should have been. There were knocked out vehicles, plenty of carts and dead Germans all over the place, many in the trees.

The main attack was towards Kleve, but we were to turn off to the right. A Company recce party and some REs started to advance down a track and came under small arms fire. It was thought that there were only a few snipers, so Major Pearson arrived and told us that a nine-man patrol, with two Vickers guns in carriers, was required to clear them out and then recce positions for the Company's machine guns. This was to prevent the enemy falling back to the south along the road that ran from Mook to Gennep, which was just inside the Dutch border. Fortunately we only had to get to a position in order to fire on the road, because the Germans had the road registered perfectly. They could land six mortars all in a line along a distance of around half a mile. They had plastered this road all day long. Lofty decided not to send in a single platoon in case they suffered heavy casualties and put it out of action, so asked for three volunteers from each platoon. I thought 'That's charming' but Frank Dollin said, '*I'll go!*' He then looked at me and said, '*You'll come with me, won't you?*' Before I could answer, he said, '*Yes, of course he'll go. Put him down!*' Sam Sleeth volunteered and a couple of others, but he had to detail the remaining few.

I was given a driver called Steadman and my carrier was to lead through a clearing in the forest, so I wanted to move down it fast, to 'bounce' the Germans out. The idea was to come onto the Germans quickly, before they had time to collect themselves and in those few seconds before they knew what was happening, open fire in an advantageous position. However, for the first and only time, the order came to attack while using the Vickers mounted on the carriers. Naturally, to fire them we were positioned high on the carriers and so were sitting ducks. I knew it was a bad idea so I said to my crew, '*If I say 'Off carrier', get off. Never mind about the order.*' We started off along the clearing, but Steadman was driving far too slowly and with one leg over the side so that he could jump out quickly. I said, '*Get a move on. You'll only make yourself an easier target by going slowly,*' but he would not. After a few hundred yards I stopped and went back to the other carrier, which was not far behind, but not so close that one shot would knock both vehicles out, and got Tommy Tubbs to come and drive my carrier. He gave me a look that could kill, but did not complain. On we went until reaching a spot where the Germans had blocked the route with felled trees. We could not get over them and a carrier was not capable of knocking a firebreak through the forest, so we came back further to another opening that was brushwood. Suddenly we came under heavy enemy *Spandau*, mortar and infantry anti-tank fire. I went back to a spot where we had passed four light Honey tanks. They did not want to come forward because of the *Panzerfaust* threat and there was no other infantry to protect them, but I did persuade one vehicle to hose the barricade area with some Bessa and shrapnel shells. Frank said to the officer, '*Well if that's the best you can do, you'd better go home. You're making the place look untidy!*' The officer replied, '*Who do you think you are talking to?*' and left. We remounted the carriers and drove back towards the barricade. We only fired a few rounds and a large amount of tracer came back at us, so I said, '*Stop*' and we got off the carriers, bringing the guns with us. The Vickers were mounted and then carrying them on their tripods, myself and Frank Dollin, and Sam

Sleeth and another chap moved alternately through the bracken, one gun firing to cover the other in rushes of about fifty yards. We could not see exactly where the fire was coming from, but I suspected that there was a pillbox about 200 yards in front. Frank and myself moved about a hundred yards to the flank and opened fire. Then suddenly, Frank was shot in the head by a sniper and fell. I went to his aid and found that the bullet had gone through his eye and out the back of his neck. He had been killed instantly. A Spandau then opened fire and a burst passed between my arm and body, tearing through the loose part of my battledress but somehow not wounding me. When you are scared you can do anything. I picked up the Vickers gun and took it back. Then, together with my remaining men, I joined a Company of Seaforth Highlanders that again attacked these enemy positions, firing into the bushes ahead of them, which I thought was rather a waste of ammunition. I was firing a *Schmeisser* taken from an enemy pillbox earlier that morning, and it had quite a rapid rate of fire, and a Seaforth officer said to me, '*Save some ammunition for when you get there.*' I had only picked up half a dozen magazines anyway. I heard a clear smack as one of the Seaforths beside me was shot and after further casualties the Seaforths were called away to join the main attack. 'Lofty' Pearson arrived and said that we could not clear the area on our own and decided not to continue, so we pulled back and just kept our eye on the enemy. Of the nine 1/7th Middlesex volunteers, two had been killed and two wounded.[6]

This position was finally cleared that night. It was found to be an enemy strongpoint with four pillboxes, defended by sixty men. As usual, no one had told the Germans they were supposed to withdraw when they saw us.

The next day, 10 February, the platoon moved forward and occupied these pillboxes, which were actually part of the Siegfried Line, in a

---

6. My good friend, Frank Dollin, aged 25, is buried in grave 55.D.3 in the Reichswald Forest War Cemetery.

position covering the Mook–Gennep road firing at withdrawing enemy transport and infantry.

Later on in the day I was walking through the wood with 'Lofty' Pearson and came across a pillbox that had a glass window. We looked at each other and he said, '*Your turn or mine?*' '*Yours.*' We were both of course armed with Webley 38 pistols, so he put a round through the window. There was a noise, so we carefully went inside. There in a bunk bed, beneath some blankets, a body was shaking. Pulling the blankets away revealed a terrified young German boy, who we took prisoner.

Our next objective was to the south and turned out to be Gennep itself, which was an important road junction. In the late afternoon of 11 February, 10 and 12 Platoon carriers loaded into amphibious assault craft known as Buffaloes to cross the area around the River Niers, which had been flooded. The bridge had been blown just as the Gordons had tried to enter the town and it could be seen collapsed in the river. The 5th Black Watch was then given the task of capturing the town and as usual they went into the assault with us following. Once in the Buffalo, you were under the command of whoever was operating it until you got out, whatever the rank of the passengers. On this occasion it was the Royal Engineers. The weather was very cold and snow was falling. Something went wrong with the navigation and we landed back almost on the same bank as we had started, which nearly caused a fight with the Royal West Kents, the infantry of the 7th Armoured Division. Finally, we got back in the Buffaloes and started off again. Shells and mortars were falling and tracer from *Spandaus* rained down on us. We landed across the flooded area but not the river. Why, I do not know. I can only guess that they had been ordered to drop us in a certain place and that is what they did. That night, Lofty Pearson said, '*We're late and I haven't had time to do a proper recce. I've got to put you in some old German trenches.*' This did not exactly please us, as the former occupants knew exactly where they were, but there was no option.

A German SP gun was firing at the collapsed bridge, which had just sunk into the river but was still crossable. This SP gun would fire and the shell would arrive almost immediately. After a while we knew how long it took for him to reload, so we rushed one across in this time gap. As soon as he fired at the bridge again, the next carrier would be off. And so one at a time we bounced across the River Niers and up the other side. I got across and our Platoon Officer went off to find out where we should be going and left me there to collect the remaining carriers as they came across, which happened just before first light. This was near the railway station, which the Germans were shelling as well, so it was not a very healthy spot to wait. Gennep underwent some heavy artillery fire and the Black Watch advanced without too much of a problem until they reached the town centre. There they met some *Fallschirmjager*, German parachutists, who had been rushed into the area. Fierce house-to-house fighting ensued and the Black Watch were heavily engaged.[7]

The fighting in Gennep lasted for thirty-six hours when at last the *Fallschirmjagers* started to pull out. We loaded the guns and everything else onto the carrier, which was positioned on the forward edge of an enemy trench and just as we started to leave, it lost a track. I could not believe it. Replacing a track was a noisy job and this would have to be done under observation. Dawn had not yet arrived but the enemy would fire towards any noise. Its design was like a bike chain, a spindle had to be knocked out, and to get the track off, a sprocket wheel at the back had to be undone and knocked forward. The track was then put back on, the spindle knocked back in and then the sprocket wheel adjusted to take up the tension. As Dennis and Harry Alcock hit the shackle pin, an enemy *Spandau* zeroed in, firing tracers. Sparks were flying off the other side of the carrier, and then it stopped. It was fortunate that the broken track was on 'our side' of the carrier.

7. Major Graham Pilcher was awarded the Military Cross during this fighting.

Harry hit it again and the machine gun fired another burst. Harry said, '*Every time I hit it, that German opens up,*' so this time he gave the pin two hits and the German responded with two bursts! Three taps were answered by three bursts. This enemy machine gunner obviously had a sense of humour. Eventually he lost interest and somehow the track stayed on long enough for the carrier to limp away a short distance for it to be put on properly.

Not long after leaving Gennep we got stuck in the mud and had to be pulled out by tanks of our old friends, the 7th Armoured Division. Eventually we moved to some high ground overlooking a valley.

At first light on 13 February the *Fallschirmjager* began evacuating wounded under Red Cross flags from a farm about 300 yards in front, which was being used as a First-Aid post. I ordered my four guns not to fire and they reached the safety of their own lines. I know we were trying to kill each other and these parachutists were pretty good at it, but they always allowed us to pick up our own wounded.

At this point our obnoxious Platoon Commander arrived with three other officers, these being a Forward Observation Officer, a Signals Officer and one from a troop of tanks to the rear. At the same time another line of Germans went across our front, obviously wounded. My corporal, who was quite new, a reinforcement, asked if he should open fire. I told him that we did not open fire at wounded soldiers under the protection of the Red Cross. Then the Platoon Commander started shouting at my corporal demanding to know why he had not opened fire. I told him '*They are all wounded and going back under the Red Cross.*' He said, '*Fire at them!*' I said, '*No. We don't fire at wounded soldiers under the protection of the Red Cross.*' So he said to the corporal. '*Open fire!*' The corporal looked at me and I said, '*Don't fire.*' The men always obey the last order. After he threatened to have us all shot at dawn, I told him that Major Pearson would have something to say about it. He then jumped behind a Vickers gun with the intention of opening fire. As described, it is impossible to fire a Vickers single-handed because of the belt needing to be hand-fed. However, he did manage two or three shots before it jammed. Everyone looked at him with contempt. Fortunately the wounded reached the safety of their own lines. I am sure the *Fallschirmjager* were not impressed by this outrageous act and it brought a heavy response down on us.

About midday a patrol of about thirty men advanced towards us. As we thought they wanted us to reveal our gun positions we did not open fire, and the Black Watch infantry were able to take care of them.

Then came an intense artillery and mortar barrage that landed all around us, and an hour after the initial attack, about 400 *Fallschirmjager* and three Tiger tanks started to advance towards us, firing their 88mm guns. I was in a forward observation trench, previously German-owned, with the Platoon Commander and the three officers, under intensive fire from the Tiger tanks who obviously had been given our position by the act described previously. One of Tigers was hit by a round from an anti-tank gun and although unable to move, continued to fire at us. One of its shells hit the parapet of our trench, to my right. The trench collapsed and the Platoon Commander was buried in the sandy soil. I was buried up to my waist and trapped, but managed to free myself enough to use my hands to keep his nose and mouth clear until other members of the platoon came forward and dug us out. The three other officers were dead.

The situation deteriorated even more when the enemy infiltrated around both flanks and our guns were under attack from all sides. To make matters even worse our own artillery, 5.5-inch mediums, started shelling us. As all our wireless sets had been destroyed, runners were sent with messages in the hope that one would get through. With our casualties mounting, we had to stand fast. There was nowhere else to go. After a couple of hours, heavy fighting could be heard to our rear and flanks and then the enemy could be seen withdrawing. They had to leave behind the Tiger with the damaged track. However, although unable to move, it was manned by a very resolute enemy crew who continued firing all through the day. The enemy recovered it that night.

On the first carrier to reach us, I saw Major 'Lofty' Pearson. I was certainly pleased to see him. Then the obnoxious Platoon Commander said to me, '*You saved my life, sergeant.*' Without thinking, I said, '*Well don't tell anyone!*' He said brusquely, '*What do you mean?*' Anyway, we 'had' him after that because he should never have given the order to open fire on the wounded Germans.

During this day's action, 10 and 12 Platoons fired 80,000 rounds. The next day, as the fighting had slackened we unwisely relaxed our vigilance and one of my blokes went missing on sentry duty. Having removed my equipment I walked about fifty yards to where 10 Platoon was dug in, to talk to my old malarial friend Alfie Littlewort. While we were talking, his cook prepared their meal. I left him spooning it out of a mess tin, and started to return to my gun. I looked to my left and to my amazement a German soldier in full marching order was walking towards us along the firebreak, looking at the ground. The following conversation subsequently took place. '*Alf, there's a bloody German walking up on you.*' Alf (still eating his dinner): '*Well leave him alone then.*' Me: '*I'm not bloody joking*'. Alf: '*Why don't you let me eat my dinner and bugger off.*' By now this German was only a few yards away and of course stupidly, having taken all my equipment off, I did not have a revolver. I stepped from behind a tree into the view of this German, who turned out to be an old boy of about forty, with his big pack on his back and a rifle over his shoulder. I shouted, '*Oi. Hande hoche* (hands up)!' He halted, looked me up and down in amazement and I shouted '*Schnell!*' He then slowly took the rifle off his shoulder, put one up the spout and aimed it at me. All the trees around were not wide enough to fully hide behind, so I had to stand sideways. He fired a shot at me and luckily, he was not the best shot in the German Army. He started moving sideways to get a shot at me and I'm gradually moving around, keeping the tree between us! He fired again and missed. At this point he decided that he had had enough, put his rifle on his shoulder and started to walk away! I think he must have been a bit bomb happy. By now my platoon had come to life. First

to arrive was an Irish bloke called Ginty O'Reilly with his Sten gun.
He always stuttered when he got excited. I said to Ginty, '*You'd better
shoot him in the leg,*' but he would never shoot anyone who was walking
away, and so he started trying to call him to halt, but only a load of
'hooing' and 'haaing' came out. We could not understand a stuttering
Irishman, so a German had no chance. Following more shouts to halt,
our German friend remained uninterested. I took Ginty's Sten, put it
on single shot, aimed it at his legs and fired. He fell to the ground. We
went over and took his equipment off, slipped his trousers down and
applied a dressing to what was a flesh wound, at the same time, trying
to tell him it was his own fault for not stopping. I then had to search
him for identity. On trying to open his left breast pocket he became
agitated, saying '*Nein, Nein.*' I thought 'He must have a few bob in
there.' However it was a photo of a woman and child. I said to him
'*Deiner Frau and Kinder?*' He replied '*Ja.*' All of us looked at it and
said '*Schon!*' It was an unwritten law that whatever you might relieve
prisoners of as the spoils of war, you always let them keep their photos,
so we put it back in his pocket. By now the stretcher-bearer had arrived
and we had to carry him a quarter of a mile to the nearest First-Aid
post, where he was given a cup of tea, and stopping for one ourselves.
We last saw him being put into an ambulance and driven away. At least
he would eventually get back home to his family, albeit with a limp.
More than some of us would.

Just as we had returned to the gun positions, we saw our Platoon
Commander approaching. He had been away when this incident took
place and had a look of thunder on his disagreeable face, so he had
obviously found out about the German prisoner. I just had time to
say to my men, '*Let me do the talking. Whatever I say, back me up.*' The
Platoon Commander said, '*What I want to know is how the German
got into our lines without being seen. Where was the sentry?*' I said, '*The
sentry reported seeing him to me and I said, 'Let him get close to make sure
of capturing him.'* He stuck his face in mine and said, '*You are a liar.*' I
turned and looked at my platoon. '*No I'm not. You ask the platoon. We*

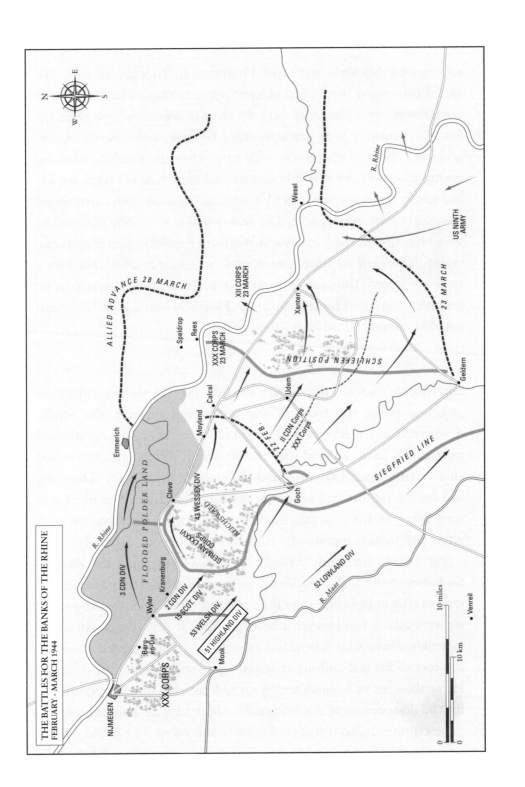

THE BATTLES FOR THE BANKS OF THE RHINE
FEBRUARY - MARCH 1944

NIJMEGEN

XXX CORPS

Berg-en-Dal

R. Rhine

Wyler
3 CDN DIV

FLOODED POLDER LAND

Kranenburg

2 CDN DIV

15 SCOT. DIV

Cleve

GERMAN LXXXVI CORPS

REICHSWALD

43 WESSEX DIV

Moyland

Calcar

Emmerich

ALLIED ADVANCE 28 MARCH

Rees

Speldrop

XXX CORPS
23 MARCH

XII CORPS
23 MARCH

Wesel

R. Rhine

US NINTH
ARMY

23 MARCH

Xanten

SCHLIEFEN POSITION

Udem

8 FEB.

II CDN Corps
XXX Corps

Goch

SIEGFRIED LINE

Gelderm

53 WELSH DIV

51 HIGHLAND DIV

Mook

R. Maas

52 LOWLAND DIV

Venrei

0   10 miles

0   10 km

all saw what happened didn't we?' He spouted, *'They are all liars, like you.'* I responded *'Well you had better report to Major Pearson that you are commanding a platoon of liars. By the way, while you're in there, tell him about ordering us to fire at wounded Germans under the Red Cross, yesterday.'* He was speechless with fury. After the incident with the enemy wounded, an invisible barrier had shut him off from us. He had totally lost our respect and I was not going to let such a person get one of my men into trouble. The sentry had done wrong (and would have been shot in the First World War) and I spoke to him afterwards, saying, *'Don't tell me where you were, I don't want to know. The least I know the better.'* Although it could have had serious consequences, he genuinely regretted his lapse of duty. I knew he was a good bloke and could be trusted not to let it happen again.

*   *   *

On 16 February we once again crossed the German frontier, the objective being the town of Goch. Passing through the totally destroyed town of Kleve on the night of 18/19 February, my platoon were going down the road with the 5th Black Watch and approached an anti-tank ditch that surrounded Goch on three sides. The town had been fully fortified as part of the Siegfried Line. The night was very foggy and it was that thick, we could not see where we were going and so were unsure of our location. Somebody decided to send a patrol down the road, through the fog, and carrying the Vickers, we followed the Jocks. Suddenly in front of us was an undefended, temporarily built bridge over the anti-tank ditch. Silently and swiftly we were across and entered a house on the far side. We discovered a German officer who was sound asleep, so he was dragged from the comfort of his bed and interrogated while still wearing his pyjamas. He spoke a bit of English and it turned out that he was responsible for the destruction of the bridge. He thought it an undignified way to be captured, plus it was cold anyway and asked if he could put his uniform on. Then he said to me, *'Can I ask you something?'* I thought he was going to ask for a fag but he said, *'Don't tell anyone I was in bed when you caught me!'* He was then happy to go to the prisoner of war camp. Unbelievably, all of his engineers were asleep in the next house!

However, next morning when the Germans found out we were there, all hell broke loose in the town. They hammered us. The house was a split-level affair, so the front was a cellar but the rear was level with the back garden. Big wooden doors led to the garden and I went out the back for something when some RAF Typhoons appeared in the sky. These swooped down and attacked us with rockets and every time I tried to open one of the doors to get back into the house, a rocket would explode and blow it shut again! This was not an unusual occurrence because all sides were attacked by Typhoons. In this house we found a big case full of *Weimar* money from before the war. Of course it was useless, but there were thousands of Marks. What was of more use were loads of jars of preservatives, fruits and things like that. We gorged ourselves on those.

A few days later, in Hekkens, just east of Gennep, 12 Platoon was badly mauled. Against their wishes, they were ordered by the Colonel of the 1st Gordons to occupy the upper floors of a big house. This was not clever as there was no way out and they were duly cut off during a German counter attack and to compound matters, a tank started shelling the building itself. A smoke screen was hastily laid down by the artillery, and ambulances rushed forward to deal with the casualties. The platoon, approximately twenty-seven strong, suffered six killed and five wounded. Alfie Littlewort had a hand blown off. The Gordons' Colonel then had the temerity to say that it was their own fault. Yet another example of an infantry officer not knowing how to best employ the Vickers.

On 21 February, the 52nd Lowland Division relieved the 51st Highland Division and two weeks later the 1/7th Middlesex Regiment returned to Gratham in Holland, to train on the River Maas for Operation *Plunder*, the assault across the River Rhine. There, we were rejoined by the 1st Northants Yeomanry, which had been trained in the use of the Buffalo. When the day came, it would be the Northants task to ferry the Highlanders across the Rhine.

The attack was fixed for 2100 hours on 23 March and our bombardment of the enemy infantry positions started at 1700 hours. 154 Brigade was to cross the near village of Honnepel on the right, 153 Brigade was to cross on either side of Ries.

Subsequently, beneath 'Monty's Moonlight', searchlights reflecting light off the cloud cover, at 2100 hours the 5th Black Watch began their crossing, followed minutes later by our carriers. The Rhine was completely obscured by a smoke screen. The boundaries of the crossing were marked by Bofors anti-aircraft guns firing green and orange lines of tracer. Each Buffalo carried one of our carriers. In our six Buffaloes of the Northants Yeomanry, we entered the water, the current of which had greatly risen and increased due to the blowing of the dams in the American sector. This caused us to cross crab-wise and although we were being shelled, it turned out to be an advantage because we were outside the worst of the enemy defensive fire. It was Dennis Daly's 21st Birthday and as this nasty stuff was landing either side of us, he quipped, *'Some bloody birthday this is!'* Downstream, nine minutes later we climbed up the far bank and reached a track. Enemy fire was intense. Leaving me to collect the six carriers, my officer pushed upstream along the bank to contact the Black Watch and to try to find our rendezvous. Having somehow all made it across we proceeded along the bank, eventually reaching where we should have landed. Our Platoon Officer had left a guide at a junction further down this road. I duly reached this junction. A Black Watch carrier had overturned and the dead crew were all around it. There were also other bodies, one of which must have been our guide. We pushed further on and I soon realized that amidst all the carnage, I did not know where we were to contact our infantry, and as there was fire coming from all directions, I pulled my little convoy alongside a hedge. There we brewed up! I had no idea where we were supposed to go and it was no use scrambling around in the dark. I knew someone would come for us. Fred Schilowski eventually arrived on his motorbike, initially so fast that he drove straight past. We were able to stop him on his way back and were informed that he was going to take us to where we were needed. As usual he flew off like a bat out of hell and that was the last we saw of him. We moved up the road, reached a big farm complex and as it was chaos, with firing going on in all directions, we drove into the courtyard of a farm to await daylight. The farm was searched and found to possess a big cellar that was full of women, old men and children. I went down there and asked if anyone could speak English and amongst them was a lady who could speak a little. I got her to reassure these frightened people, that if they stayed where they were no one would harm them. They had a hurricane lamp and as we were walking out, one of my blokes picked it up. I said, '*What are you doing?*' He said, '*We could do with this.*' I said, '*We can't leave all these people sitting in the dark. They're frightened out of their lives now.*' So he gave it back. One good deed for the day.

In the morning we were collected. Our immediate objective was the village of Esserden, and after an unsuccessful attack on Speldrop, turned right towards Ries. It was then we heard the planes of the approaching 6th Airborne and 17th US Airborne Divisions who started dropping to our right. The enemy put up a terrific barrage. At one time, in my area of vision I could see five planes coming down on fire. They must have suffered heavy casualties. It was at this stage that the jeep carrying our Divisional Commander, General Tom Rennie, received a direct hit from a mortar bomb. He was taken to 176 Field Ambulance, which was only thirty yards away, but died immediately.

After capturing Ries our next objective was Anholt. After another sharp fight a river was crossed to Dinxperlo, a border village, half in the Netherlands and half in Germany. The arrival of our tanks made the Germans fall back. In twenty-four hours 27,000 shells were fired into it. Some liberation.

In Dinxperloo, we were billeted in a house owned by Karel and Ria Baayens. One morning, when I was elsewhere, there was a real hullabaloo. Major Carter was in the bath and began shouting for help. He could not get out because of his wound, even though it had been sustained over a year ago. Karel could not take his wife in there for obvious reasons, so he had to run down the road to get a neighbour to help lift him out!

* * *

For about ten days there was some terrific fighting in the villages beyond the Rhine. When the infantry were sorting something out, the tracer bullets would be flying by. The carriers only had thin armour that might stop a bullet at extreme range and everyone would have to sit there with their head and shoulders above the top. I would hang on to the bottom of the seat. Dennis would be sitting there saying, '*Have you got me lost again?*'

A problem that occurred during the last few months had been the supply of what was called streamlined ammunition. I believe it came from Canada and was supposed to give extra range. It was obviously still .303 inch, but we were getting quite a few misfires.

On 4 April 10 Platoon moved to Enschede. From now on it was to be Germany only. Resistance was sporadic and we quickly advanced twenty miles east to Salzbergen, then north-east thirty miles to Quakenbrucken, eighteen miles to Vechta, a further eighteen miles to Wilderhausen. Then on 20 April, we reached Delmenhorst, about ten miles from Bremen. Here I received a message that the Colonel wanted to see me. As ever, my immediate reaction was 'What have I done now?' I went into his office and standing there he said, '*Sergeant, I've got some good news for you. You've been awarded the Military Medal.*' I could not think what for. Did they have the right bloke? '*What was that for Colonel?*' He told me what it was for the action in the *Reichswald* and I said '*Well I didn't think it deserved a medal.*' He said, '*Well done. Carry on the good work.*' I am sure there were many others, equally deserving, whose bravery and courage went unnoticed or unrewarded. Major

Pearson himself had been awarded a bar to his Military Cross for his actions in leading the relief column at Gennep.

* * *

The inexorable advance continued towards our final objective of Bremerhaven, about twenty-five miles away. It was about this time that 'my bad apple driver' once again showed his true colours and let himself and everyone else down. At the time the 5th Black Watch had been attacking a village all day, unable to capture it. We waited in the grounds of a large house to be called forward and all day the wounded of both sides had been coming down the road past us. We were eventually told that my platoon would move forward at 2200 hours under cover of darkness. It was a long time to wait and waiting was the worst part of any attack. When the time came to line up our carriers to move forward this driver was missing. Dennis Daly therefore put this carrier in its correct place. Together with my officer we carried out a search, going down a particular cellar that contained a large pile of coal. We saw movement and found him hiding amongst it. He refused to leave the cellar saying, '*I don't want to get killed.*' As if any of us did. We pulled him out and physically sat him in the driving seat of his carrier. Nothing could convince him to change his mind. He had a wife and child in England. I said to him, '*What will your family think of you letting every one down?*' He said, '*I don't care what you say or do, I'm not driving up that road.*' The Company Commander arrived and as it was time for us to move forward, he had no option other than to order him to be taken back. He was put into a spare carrier under the guard of Sergeant Fred Addison while Dennis drove them back to Company HQ.

This now left my carrier with no driver, so although not officially qualified, from my previous experience I knew enough to get along the road. We advanced to the forward positions of the Black Watch, to find that it had been decided to postpone the next attack until first light. Meanwhile Dennis, having delivered the prisoner, was returning to us. As there was no other form of light in the forward area, direction was maintained by punching holes in disused petrol tins standing over a hurricane lamp. As Dennis reached the forward Black Watch infantry, the lamp was being filled with paraffin and so was not alight. Dennis and Fred sped past in a rattle of tracks, straight into the village we had been trying to capture all day. After passing a few houses, a door opened and some armed German soldiers walked out. I don't know who would have been the more surprised, them or the Germans. Quickly realizing the situation, Dennis swung the carrier round, which he could do in its own length by stopping one track, while Fred threw a couple of Mills 36 grenades and they managed to disappear into the night. Their next problem was to get to our lines without being shot by the Black Watch. However, they had witnessed Dennis and Fred's attempt to capture the village on their own and had lit the lamp to show their positions, surmising it was them coming back. The outcome was that everyone had a good laugh at their expense. Later that night the Germans withdrew from the village and we entered it next morning without opposition.

At this stage of the fighting, with the end of the war now in sight, resistance was unpredictable.

Sometimes the advance would be many miles a day against German units who had seen the writing on the wall and were willing to give up, and other days having to fight for every yard against an enemy determined to carry on to the last. We were passing through German towns that were not too badly damaged and in one of them, Queckenburgh, the bank was still standing and contained a large safe. Of course you do all sorts of silly things and we thought there might be a few bob in it and decided to open it with a Projectile Infantry Anti-Tank [PIAT] which fired a solid shot and had a kick-back like a mule. Sergeant Major Waller appeared and decided he wanted a share of the loot, and would fire the PIAT himself. He laid down and aimed at the safe at the other end of the room. We persuaded him that all he would do was kill himself with the blast, so he took it outside and standing on a thin, wooden slatted box, aimed the PIAT through the window. The rest of us stood back a safe distance and looked on with interest. He fired the PIAT and there was an almighty bang and a cloud of smoke, followed by our gallant Sergeant Major being blown back down the road. Everyone entered the bank. The PIAT had certainly opened the safe door. Inside were scraps of charred paper and a few unidentifiable items fused together by the explosion. The only reward for our trouble was the Sergeant Major being out of action for a few days with a dislocated shoulder!

*   *   *

Mutual agreement was reached through the auspices of the Red Cross to neither attack nor defend, but of course there were still casualties occurring. At this stage an 'incident' did occur. My platoon was occupying an empty textile mill. As we were bored we decided to fight each other with bags of white powder used for dying cloth. We had made quite a mess, when at the entrance appeared two German gentlemen, telling us that they were the owners and we had to stop damaging their factory. After telling them in plain English what to do, one of my boys dropped a bag from an upstairs window on them, scoring a direct hit. They withdrew. Later, they reappeared with a Staff Major, who tore us off a strip. I told him, *'After murdering their way across Europe and back, they are worrying about a bag of powder!'* This Major ordered us out of the factory. 'Lofty' Pearson then appeared. I think he had a twinkle in his eye when he heard of the white powder 'bombing' of the Germans. However the Staff Major gave him an order that my platoon was never to be allowed to sleep in German houses as we could not be trusted. Sometime later 'Lofty' showed us a written order to this effect. However, being the kind of man he was, he said, *'If they think I'm going round every night to see where you have tucked yourselves in, they have another bloody thing coming.'*

*   *   *

Bremerhaven was now only a short distance away. Together with the 5th Black Watch we crossed a small river called the Ost and the following afternoon, on 7 May, my platoon was supporting them by firing on a wood. One of their officers approached me and said, '*Order your guns to cease fire, the war is over tomorrow, but we have reached a local agreement with the Germans opposite to save lives by ceasing fire at once.*' The actual stipulated time turned out to be eight o'clock the following morning. Everyone was told not to fire except in self-defence. Both sides retired three kilometres so there would not be any idiots doing anything that night. That same feeling returned again. I could not believe it was all over and that I was still alive. With nothing stronger being available with which to celebrate, we all had a cup of tea.

Then 'Lofty' appeared and said, '*Come back to the Company Headquarters and if you happen to run over a few German chickens on the way, we'll have them for dinner.*' With the war over, we thought it might be better to get them from the farms outside our area, so we went to a farm further down the road. A few of us got into the chicken coop and wrung all these chicken's necks. When we got back we found that someone had pinched all the chickens from our area! For something to drink, an old German was bribed with fags, and some *Kartoffel Schnapps*, manufactured from potatoes, was obtained. Everyone began drinking it, a mugful at a time. Unfortunately, it had a delayed effect and after a while I knew I was going to pass out. The platoon was sleeping in this house, so I went upstairs and lay on the floor while I was still capable. Meanwhile, everyone became ill and it descended into a brawl, with the chicken dinner remaining uneaten. A chap called Roy Holmwood must have drunk even more than anyone else and when everybody woke up the next morning with blinding headaches, he was still unconscious and had soiled himself. Dennis and Harry cleaned him up and he was placed in a truck with the windscreen wide open and driven around in order to try and sober him up. He came around but only really giggled and said he had no feeling in his arms. They took him to the Field Hospital and left him there to be attended to. A couple of days later, 'Lofty' informed us that he had died. He had fought right through the war and had been a good soldier.

*   *   *

10 Platoon were ordered to smarten up ourselves and the carriers. The 15th Panzer Grenadier Division had asked to surrender to the Highland Division, which in theory it had fought all the way from Alamein. This was a reconstituted Division because the original had been captured in North Africa. It was now part of the Korps Ems and the General in question, Rasp, was worried that he did not have total control of some of the units under his command, namely the SS and Hitler Youth. Apparently our General said, '*Disarm your best and most reliable unit last.*' His most reliable was the 15th Panzer Grenadier Division. My platoon, about thirty of us, had to take a Company of this Division. These were all lined up in a field. The orders were to take away anything that might be used as a weapon. I said to my blokes, '*Don't forget, you are soldiers, not thieves.*' As we went along the lines, the Germans looked at me as if to say, 'How did this shower ever win the war?' Some of my men were taking their knives and forks, so I said, '*What are you doing? How are they going to eat their grub without any eating irons?*' I started walking behind my group, giving the Germans all their knives and forks back! The Germans thought it was hilarious. I found a German *Kriegsmarine* bloke that could speak good English and told him he was going to be my interpreter. He said, '*I'll have to ask my officer first.*' I said, '*Don't ask him. Tell him. You'll be riding with me, so you won't have to walk.*' He must have thought, 'That's not bad!' I told him to tell the men that they were just going to be documented and then sent home. I did not know what was going to happen with them, but all I was worried about was getting them where they were meant to go! They all marched out of the field in order singing, '*Deutschland uber Alles.*' We had these prisoners for three days and got on all right with them.

On the third day, the *Kriegsmarine* bloke said, '*Can I ask you something, sergeant? If one of the prisoners ran away, would you really shoot him?*' '*Why are you asking that?*' He said, '*One of them lives near here and he wants to run away.*' I said, '*I think he's bloody silly because if he waits a few days he'll get his discharge papers and get home legitimately.*' He replied, '*He wants to go home and see his wife.*' I said, '*All right. You tell me when he's going to run and I'll look the other way.*' So he passed the word around and I saw this bloke harping across the field. When we got to the destination I was asked if I had lost any. I said, '*I've lost one.*' Lofty said, '*Well where did he go?*' I said, '*If I knew that I wouldn't have lost him!*' Laughing, he said, '*I suppose not.*' I said to this *Kriegsmarine* interpreter, '*Do you know, you Germans are a bloody nuisance.*' He said, '*Yes!*' We never had any trouble with those prisoners at all.

On 14 June I travelled to a place near Hamburg called Stade, to a former *Luftwaffe* base. It was here that the medal ribbon presentation was taking place and the ceremony was to be performed by none other than Field Marshal Bernard Montgomery himself. It was all done in what looked like a cinema that had a stage. A Jock officer in a kilt was stood there with a list and he sorted out everyone into the order on his list. Apart from a medical chap getting the DCM, everyone was being awarded the MM. Monty took up position in the centre of the stage, and the officer began calling out the names. When he called my name, I walked over to Monty from the side of the stage, came to attention, saluted and he returned the salute. He pinned the ribbon on me and just said '*Well done.*' I saluted him again and walked off to opposite side of the stage. During the presentation, everyone had their photograph taken, but I found that when it had come to my turn, the photographer was changing his film! However, afterwards everyone went outside and a group photograph was taken.

Subsequently, there was a Victory Parade in Bremerhaven but I finished as I started, and managed to avoid it and watched from the side of the road.

* * *

A few weeks after the war had ended, I had to attend a Court-Martial, the only time in all my years as an NCO I had to charge anybody. The errant driver 'F' faced the reduced charge of failing to comply with an order, instead of refusing to obey an order. He was sentenced to three years detention. However, in general they usually only served half of the sentence.

*   *   *

During the period since the war had ended, everyone had been billeted in houses and began handing them back. I said to the German interpreter, '*If you tell these people to say they're not going to claim against the British Army for damage, they can have their houses back straight away, but if they are going to make a nuisance of themselves, they can't.*' It was just to cover for the odd broken chair and suchlike. However, one of them said, '*No*' and complained. A bloke from the Control Commission came along with an underling, both in some sort of uniform and asked '*Are you Sergeant Haward?*' '*Yes.*' '*Well I want a word with you.*' '*What about?*' '*You've been threatening these Germans about getting their rooms back.*' I looked at him as if he was something unpleasant I had trodden in and said, '*Look here. These Germans have murdered and smashed their way across Europe and back. Now they're worried because they've got a broken chair leg! You take these lists and you do it.*' He said, '*You can't talk to me like that.*' '*Well I just have!*' I saw Lofty Pearson approaching and so I said to this bloke, '*Here's my Company Commander. Go and complain to him.*' Off he went, all full of himself, and repeated what I'd said. Pearson replied '*I'd have said the same if it was me! Don't bother me!*'

*   *   *

The battalion moved to Haserfeld, into a *Kriegsmarine* barracks and spent a year in Germany before being finally pulled out for a move to the north German coast. However, a few men were due for demobilization and I was one of them. When the 1/7th Middlesex marched out of the barracks, the Colonel was in front, leading the column in a 15cwt truck. On reaching the end of the village, he stopped the vehicle, called me over, shook hands and said, '*I wish you all good luck in civilian life.*'

Together with Sergeants Addison and Lamborn [both MM] I spent a night in Hanover and subsequently sailed home. The first night back in England was spent in Shornecliff and the next day, 24 April 1946, it was demob at Olympia in London, walking in as a soldier and out as a civvy. It was a huge store from which everyone picked all their civilian clothes. Outside, the spivs were waiting to buy this clothing, coupon-free demob suits.

After my demob leave finished, I received a letter from the Regimental Paymaster at Knightsbridge stating that I had served for 2,315 days and had been overpaid by one day. Therefore, I was required to pay back ten shillings and tenpence.

Chapter Ten

Post-War

When I got home I found that only three of my four mates had come back from the war. The one who had not was John Suddes, who had gone out to the Far East. Charlie Howard had been in the Royal Air Force and survived many bombing raids. He had got married during the war and so did not live in the street any more, but upon my return, the remaining four of us went out. As we walked past Suddes' house, his father came running out. He asked if we had any idea what had happened to his son. All I could say was that I had not been out to the Far East, so I could not tell him anything about it. The other two had both served in Italy, but I did say, '*People are turning up all the time, so don't give up hope.*' He was naturally upset. I did not want to prolong his agony, so I just said, '*I'm sorry I can't help you,*' and we walked on.

I found out later that just as Singapore was about to be surrendered, a troop ship had been approaching the island. The Japanese stated that as part of the surrender, the ship had to come in, so all of these troops marched straight into captivity and my mate Suddes was amongst them. He was never heard from again. It would appear from the Commonwealth War Graves Commission records that he died on the 4th August 1943, eighteen months after the Singapore fiasco. He is buried in the Thanbyuzayat Cemetery in Burma, which contains many men who died while building the Burma – Siam Railway.

* * *

I went to live with my sister in North London but due to the lack of space, moved to her mother and father-in-law's place as they had a spare room. After a short spell back doing some plumbing, I decided to go on the buses, initially becoming a conductor, then a driver at Potter's Bar Garage.

In 1947, I met Ivy Ades in the canteen and we seemed to get on all right. She was in digs as well, as she came from south east London. Ivy had been in the Land Army and upon leaving had got a job on the buses and been sent to Potter's Bar. We obviously liked each other and so went out on a date. All I had in my pocket was ten shillings. That first night she turned up wearing a fur coat and I thought 'I'm all right here. She must have a few bob!' I found out afterwards that she had borrowed it from her landlady! We agreed to go out with each other for six months and if we were still talking, see about taking it further. And so six months later, we went to her parents house in Ancona Road, Plumstead, and met her mother and father. I said to her father '*I want to ask if you have any objection to me asking your daughter to marry me.*' He was a dry old stick and said, '*Objection? I'm bloody glad to get rid of her!*'

We were married for forty-three years and had two sons, John and Keith. We lost her in 1992.

Chapter Eleven

Return to Normandy

In June 1994 I returned to Normandy for the first time to specifically look at the area around which I had served. I was a little concerned because it had always been on my mind that perhaps the French would not be very welcoming after Normandy had been left in such a ruined state.

I travelled with my nephew, Neil Barber, two weeks after what had been the memorable 50th Anniversary of D-Day. This was done deliberately to avoid the chaos of that week.

Armed with the 1/7th Middlesex War Diary and actual battle maps from the period, we began to trace the locations at which my Vickers was positioned. This was to lead to the most extraordinary sequence of events and coincidences.

We had driven to the *Butte de la Hogue*, one of the 6th Airborne Division Drop Zones during the early hours of D-Day. The battle map was laid out on the bonnet and we were analysing the area when from nowhere, a vivacious jogger approached, stopped and enquired if we were lost. After explaining what we were doing and why, she said that her parents were very interested in the war and would love to meet me. They lived in the nearby village of Cuverville, which had been in the front line of the German defences, opposite the initial Airborne perimeter. Arriving in the village we met what turned out to be Maurice and Roland Dufour. They kindly invited us in for a drink and an interesting conversation, particularly as our French was poor and their English was non-existent. As we were leaving, Neil went over to what appeared to be a newly unveiled monument. To his amazement, it was dedicated to the Middlesex Regiment. This was quite a surprise, especially as we were not sure if any Middlesex battalion had served in that area!

Then the story began to unfold. The village had wanted to do something to show their appreciation to the fallen for the 50th Anniversary of D-Day. It was well known in the village that there had been two bodies of British soldiers buried in the back garden of a farmhouse owned by a Madame Marie Fernard. They had been killed on 18 July 1944 while supporting the Monmouths during the advance through Cuverville during Operation *Goodwood*. After the war, she refused to allow them to be moved to an official cemetery. The names of these two men were Harold Luxton and Martin Philbin. When Madame Fernard passed away, they were moved to Ranville cemetery, but the lady's grandson, Andre Cenedese, had maintained shrines on the spot where they were originally buried. Even the wall, which had been damaged during the fighting, had been left as it was.

The village had traced Harold Luxton's wife, Joyce, daughter Mary and two sons John and Harold. They were located in Australia and travelled over for the ceremony on 6 June that year.

Subsequent to this, our little Middlesex group of Alan Carter, Dennis Daly, Bill Jones, Arthur Berry (RA) and myself became very attached to Cuverville and for a memorable few years, every July during the day of their liberation, we would be welcomed with open arms and Calvados. On one occasion we donated a Vickers machine gun, which can still be seen in the Cuverville Town Hall.

It is marvellous to know that the Middlesex has a permanent memorial in Normandy.

*   *   *

Writing this in February 2014, other than myself there is only one known member left of my true and trustworthy friends of those years. He is my wireless operator, Ken Thiis. The rest, like all old soldiers, have simply faded away.

And finally, the Regimental Paymaster is still waiting for his ten shillings and tenpence.

*   *   *

Index